The Campaign in Holland, 1799

DUKE OF YORK

The Campaign in Holland, 1799

The British/Russian Expedition Against the Gallo/Batavian Forces in the Low Countries

A Subaltern

LEONAUR

The Campaign in Holland, 1799
The British/Russian Expedition Against the
Gallo/Batavian Forces in the Low Countries
by A Subaltern

First published under the title
The Campaign in Holland, 1799

Leonaur is an imprint of Oakpast Ltd

Copyright in this form © 2011 Oakpast Ltd

ISBN: 978-0-85706-615-2 (hardcover)
ISBN: 978-0-85706-616-9 (softcover)

http://www.leonaur.com

Publisher's Notes

Contents

Introduction

The object of the following pages is to give a fair and impartial account of the Duke of York's Campaign in Holland, in the year 1799. The naval successes obtained on the occasion of the Expedition to the Texel have been fully described in the different Naval Histories; but I believe that there is no military history which gives a description of the subsequent military operations, in such detail as to be at all commensurate with the importance of the subject. In the compilation of the following pages, an attempt has been made to supply this deficiency, by consulting the Naval and Military Magazines, the files of the *Moniteur*, and other contemporary publications and periodicals, also the official dispatches of the hostile Commanders-in-Chief, and the Military History of Jomini.

Fort Manoel, Malta,
23rd October, 1861.

TEXEL

EIERLAND

den Burg
Oude-Schild
Hoorn

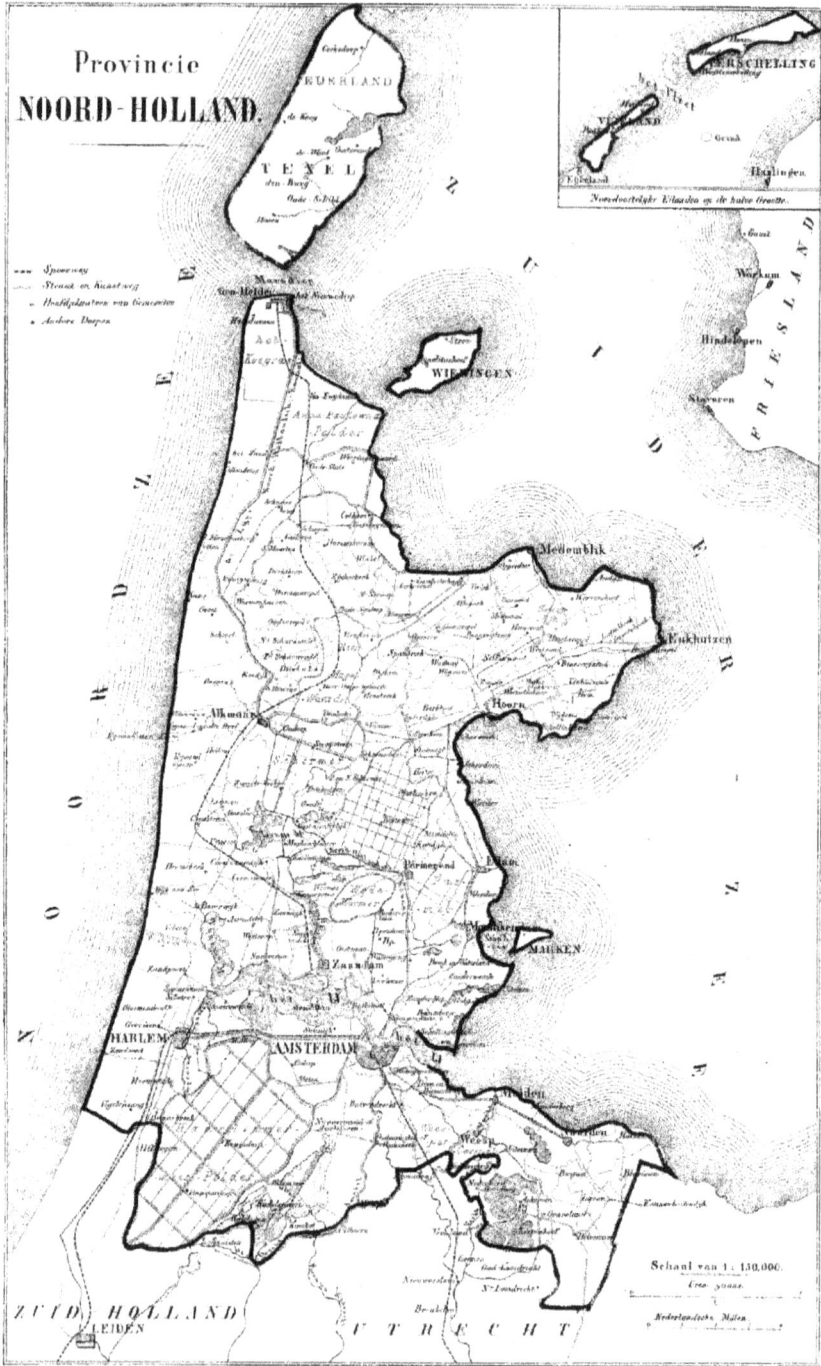

Spoorweg
Straat en Kunstweg
Hoofdplaatsen van Gemeenten
Andere Dorpen

Nieuwediep
Helder

WIERINGEN

Anna Paulowna Polder

Medemblik

Enkhuizen

Alkmaar

Hoorn

Beverwijk

Edam

Zaandam

MARKEN

HAARLEM

AMSTERDAM

Weesp

ZUIDERZEE

FRIESLAND

Workum

Hindelopen

Stavoren

TERSCHELLING

VLIELAND

Griend

Harlingen

Noordoostelijke Eilanden op de halve Grootte.

ZUID HOLLAND

LEIDEN

UTRECHT

Schaal van 1 : 150,000.

Nederlandsche Mijlen

CHAPTER 1

The Campaign Begins

In the summer of the year 1799, the British Ministry came to a resolution to send an army into Holland, with the view of driving out the French, overturning the Republican Government established under their protection, and bringing the country once more under the dominion of the House of Orange and Stadtholderat. On the Continent, all things seemed favourable to the success of such an undertaking; for, during the last few weeks, the French army, under Jourdan, had been defeated by the Austrian Archduke Charles, in a succession of battles between the Danube and the Lake of Constance, driven out of Suabia, and compelled to repass the Rhine, while Massena was hard pressed in Switzerland; and the whole of Italy, with the exception of the maritime fortress of Genoa, had been overrun by the Austrian and Russian armies, under Melas and Suwarrow. The appearance of a powerful British army in Holland would, it was considered, effect an important diversion in favour of the allied armies now operating against the French Republic, by forcing the Government of the latter to send to the assistance of their Batavian allies a great part of the troops hitherto destined to reinforce their army of the Rhine.

Acting on these considerations, therefore, the Government of King George the Third lost no time in opening negotiations with the Emperor Paul the First of Russia, with a view to obtain from him the assistance of an auxiliary corps of Russian troops in the contemplated expedition. This Prince entered heartily into their plans, being of opinion that the deliverance of Holland from the power of France would have a decided influence on the results of the war; and, on the 22nd of June, a treaty was concluded, by which he agreed to furnish a force of seventeen battalions of infantry, two companies of artillery, one company of pioneers, and one squadron of hussars, amounting in the whole to 17,593 men.

For the service of these 17,593 troops. Great Britain was to pay to Russia the sum of £88,000 sterling— one half to be paid when they should be ready to embark at Revel, and the other three months later; also a subsidy of £44,000 a month, to be computed from the day the troops were ready. Horses were to be furnished for their officers, artillery, and baggage; while, in case the Russian troops should be unable to return to their own country before the ensuing cold season, Great Britain was to find them good quarters in her own dominions. In order to provide for the conveyance of a portion of his troops, the Emperor of Russia undertook to furnish six ships of the line, five frigates, and two large transports, all armed *en flûte*; the remainder were to embark on board English or other transport vessels freighted by His Britannic Majesty.[1]

On their side, the British Government bound themselves, by this treaty concluded with the Emperor of Russia, to contribute 13,000 troops—or, at least, 8,000, should the smaller number be deemed sufficient, to include a proportion of cavalry sufficient for the service of so large an army. They also proposed to support by their fleets the operations of the combined forces. Strange as it may appear, the assembling even of 8,000 troops in this country would have been, a few months before, a task of almost insuperable difficulty. This unfortunate state of things was attributable to a succession of causes reaching as far back as the commencement of the Revolutionary War in 1793.

At that time the British army was made up of mere skeleton regiments, expensive in time of peace and most inefficient in actual service, as was proved in Flanders, whither all such as could

---

1. See Appendix No, 1, for details concerning the Russian. Contingent.

be spared were sent to assist the Austrians. They behaved well as often as they met the enemy, but the hardships of a retreat in the depth of a severe winter told severely on troops unused, as they were, to shift for themselves in the field. Such regiments as remained after the conclusion of the last disastrous campaign were at once shipped off to the West Indies, to effect the reduction of the French and Spanish islands; and while thus engaged, the men died by thousands.[2] Thus it came to pass, that, by the end of 1795, there was scarcely any regular army at all. To fill up the vacuum, recourse was then had to the system of raising men for rank, which opened a field to the most disgraceful traffic without effecting the object in view. In a short time, indeed, there were no less than 135 regiments of infantry alone on paper—for officers anxious to obtain rank took almost any men who offered; nor were those who passed the recruits more particular. Hundreds of men made a regular trade of enlisting to receive the bounty in one regiment, and then deserting to play the same game over again in another.

This system was put a stop to by the Duke of York as soon as he came into command, for, on perceiving all its evils in their full force, he caused all the new regiments, numbered from the 101st, or Fullerton's, to the 136th, or Hunt's Limerick, to be reduced, and their few effective men draughted to the skeleton regiments sent home about this time from the West Indies. After an unsuccessful attempt, made in 1796, to induce the rank and file of the supplementary regiments of militia to volunteer, the army remained, until 1799, in the lowest possible state of efficiency. As an instance of the incomplete state of regiments at this time, the 6th Royals could only bring 120 men into the field at Castlebar.

At length, early in the year 1799, Mr. Pitt brought a Bill be-

2. From the 1st March, 1796, to the end of 1799, there died, in the Leeward Islands, 2 brigadier-generals, 19 lieutenant-colonels, 12 majors, 72 captains, 169 subalterns, 11 adjutants, 9 quartermasters, 14 surgeons, 19 assistant-surgeons, and 14,327 non-commissioned officers and men, besides about 187 of the latter belonging to draughted regiments, who were left, in July, 1796, in the different hospitals. This frightful mortality was greatest in St Lucia and Grenada.

fore Parliament, by which one-fourth of the effective strength of every militia regiment were to be permitted to volunteer into the line; and this Bill he succeeded in carrying, in spite of serious opposition on the part of some lord-lieutenants of counties and of the militia colonels, who had an interest in keeping the regiments intact. This measure proved most successful, for the militiamen came forward in thousands, their military ardour being greatly excited by the preparations already set on foot for the expedition to Holland. On the 12th of July, a squadron under Captain Sir Home Popham had sailed for Revel, there to embark the Russian auxiliary troops, while a considerable corps, formed of regiments drawn from Ireland and the Channel Islands, was encamped on Shirley Common, near Southampton, under the orders of Lieutenant-General Sir Ralph Abercromby.

Towards the end of July this corps was moved to Barham Downs, situated about four miles from Canterbury, on the high road to Dover, where the volunteers from the militia began to come in; and in three weeks after, several regiments which had come into camp with scarcely 300 rank and file, found themselves with 1,700 or 1,800 on their muster rolls, and were consequently obliged to form second battalions; while the 4th and the 9th, being favourite regiments, were enabled to form three each.[3]

For some time, considerable doubt had existed in the councils of the British Government as to the part of Holland where a disembarkation could be effected to most advantage. Most military men were of opinion that the landing should take place near the mouth of the Meuse, or on the side of Terheyde or Scheveningen, with a view to the occupation of the Hague, in which city the partisans of the *Stadtholder* formed a numerous and influential party. From the Hague the expeditionary force would threaten the line of communication between the French troops to the northward and their own country, and the least success obtained over them would probably cause Amsterdam to hoist Orange colours, and throw open its gates to the British

---

3. See Appendix No. 2, for distribution of the British army at this period.

as deliverers.

Finally, however, the peninsula of the Helder, forming the northern extremity of the province of North Holland, was selected, from the circumstance of its shores being more easy of access than the rest of the Dutch coast, which is nearly everywhere fringed with dangerous reefs and sandbanks.

Moreover, in North Holland there were no strong fortresses, and a few weak coast batteries constituted its only defences; while, once in possession of the Helder, the seizure of the Dutch fleet lying in the Texel Roads would become a comparatively easy task for the British commanders, and the fate of the war might be subsequently decided by a successful advance on Amsterdam.

On the Continent the destination of the expedition now preparing in Great Britain soon became known, since the British Ministry, never doubting of success, took no pains whatever to conceal it, and, on their side, the Batavian Government determined to spare no pains to give the invading army the warmest possible reception. Their newly-formed army, however, comprised but 20,000 men of all arms—an inconsiderable force with which to attempt the defence of the coast line of seven provinces. General Daendels, an officer of some experience, who had been appointed to command the whole, was posted in North Holland with the first division, while the second, under General Dumonceau, was stationed in Friesland, the country about Groningen, and on the frontiers of Overyssel.

By the treaty of alliance with France, the Republic of Holland was also entitled to the support of an army of 24,000 French troops; but of these only 15,000 were at hand, the recent reverses which had befallen their arms having put it out of the power of the Directory to send the number promised, while those they had sent were of a very inferior description, being from the last levies of the conscription, undersized and half drilled. A portion lay between Nimeguen and the sea, and the remainder, under General Desjardins, guarded the islands of Zealand.

As soon, however, as the prospects of invasion became imminent, the formation at Liège of a camp, to be occupied by some old French battalions stationed in Belgium, and by a certain number of auxiliary battalions raised in the Northern Departments, was ordered; the command of this corps was given to General Tilly, with instructions to guard against any rising of the Belgian partisans of the House of Orange. The fortifications of Walcheren and at the mouths of the Scheldt, where it was thought likely the British might attempt to land, were repaired and strengthened, and a number of gunboats were fitted out to support General Desjardins in the Isles of Zealand. To the French general, Brune, was given, at the express request of the Batavian Government, the chief command of all the French and Dutch troops intended for the defence of Holland.

Meanwhile, the British Government, finding that it would be almost impossible to cause troops still cantoned round Bevel, to arrive at the same time off the coast of Holland, as others spread over the southern counties of England (particularly as a north wind was indispensably necessary to bring the Russians down from the Baltic, while a south wind was equally necessary to carry the British fleets into the North Sea), decided not to waste time in waiting for the former, but at once to send on Abercromby's division, conveyed by a squadron under Vice-Admiral Mitchell; this division to be followed a short time after by another, under the Duke of York, who was to take command of the whole army.

Under favourable circumstances, it was calculated that the Russians would arrive at about the same time as the Duke of York's division; and, in the interval, it was confidently anticipated that Sir Ralph Abercromby, favoured by the nature of the country and supported by the fleet, would be able to maintain his ground. Accordingly, by the 8th of August, the troops composing this officer's division were assembled in and about the ports of Margate, Ramsgate, Deal, and Dover, where they were ordered to embark. The whole force, amounting to about 11,900 men, was divided into four brigades and a reserve, as follows:—

1st Brigade, under Major-General D'Oyley: The 3rd battalion 1st Foot Guards and a flank battalion of grenadier companies of the Guards, which had been formed early in 1798 for service in Ireland, by taking two companies each from the 1st and 2nd battalions 1st Foot Guards, and two companies each from the Coldstreams and 3rd Foot Guards.

2nd Brigade, under Major-General Burrard: The 1st battalions of the Coldstream and 3rd regiment of Guards. These four battalions were all between 900 and 1,000 strong.

3rd Brigade, under Major-General Coote: The 2nd or Queen's, 27th, 29th, 69th, and 85th regiments. Of these regiments, the 2nd (596 strong) and the 29th (630 strong) had served in Ireland during the Rebellion of the previous year, and only landed at Southampton from Cork in July; the 27th (868 strong) had come home this year from Grenada; while the 69th had recently been serving on board the fleet as marines, and in that capacity were greatly distinguished in the Battle of Cape St. Vincent. The 85th, although comparatively a young regiment—having only been raised in 1793—had already seen service in the very country to which it was now proceeding; coming direct from Jersey, it joined the rest of the expedition in the Downs.

4th Brigade, under Major-General Moore: 2nd battalion 1st Royals, 596 strong; 25th regiment, 501; 49th regiment, 461; 79th Highlanders, 780; and 92nd Highlanders, 792. Of these regiments, the Royals had come home in June from Portugal, and the 25th had returned a perfect skeleton from the West Indies in September, 1796. The 49th had also come home from Jamaica in March of the latter year, and the 79th from the West Indies in August, 1797, while the 92nd had come from Ireland with the 2nd and 29th. The 25th, 49th, and 79th, were all brought from

Guernsey to the camp near Southampton in June, 1799.

The Reserve, which was more particularly attached to the 3rd Brigade, was formed of the 23rd Royal Welsh Fusiliers (905 effectives) and the 55th regiment, with two squadrons of the 18th Light Dragoons, under Colonel Macdonald of the 55th. Of the two infantry regiments, the 23rd had come home very weak from St. Domingo in 1796; in 1798, its flank companies were made prisoners, together with the rest of the troops engaged in the unfortunate expedition to Ostend. The 55th had arrived in England from the West Indies, after serving among the islands, and being draughted, on the 18th July, 1797.

Both the 23rd and 55th were brought from Guernsey, to join the camp at Barham Downs. Portions of the 3rd and 4th battalions Royal Artillery, under Lieutenant-Colonel Whitworth, and a party of the Royal Engineers, under Lieutenant-Colonel Hay, accompanied the army; but the Medical Staff was insufficient, and there was no regular Commissariat Staff. The Head-Quarters Staff was formed of Lieutenant-General Sir James Pulteney, as second in command; Lieutenant-Colonel the Hon. John Hope, as Deputy Adjutant-General; Lieutenant-Colonel Alexander Hope, Assistant Adjutant-General; and Lieutenant-Colonel Anstruther, Deputy Quarter-master-General.

From the 9th to the 12th of August was occupied in embarking the troops on board the hired transports and men-of-war, armed *en flûte*, and fitted up for their reception; and on the morning of the 13th, the entire fleet, consisting of 200 sail of square-rigged vessels, and 11 luggers and cutters, with 50 flat-bottomed boats for landing men, sailed from Deal for its destination, under the conduct of Vice-Admiral Mitchell, in the 50-gun ship, *Isis*. At first the weather seemed propitious, but during the 14th it became so stormy that the fleet was compelled to alter its course. Next day it encountered the North Sea Fleet, which had been for some time on a cruise, when the admiral,

Lord Duncan, separated himself from his command in his flag-ship, the *Kent*, 74, and came on with the expedition.

At noon a south-westerly gale came on, and continued to blow, almost incessantly, during the next five days. During this stormy weather, most unusual for the time of year, many of the ships of war and transports were much damaged, and the whole fleet considerably scattered. On the 20th the gale was followed by a calm. Next day, however, the wind became favourable, and the whole fleet stood in towards the Dutch coast, and anchored by signal, in the evening, within five miles of the Texel Roads and two of the shore. It was then decided to effect a landing next morning, for which purpose the transports weighed anchor early on the 22nd, in order to take up a more convenient position within half a mile of the shore, and the small vessels and flat-bottomed boats made ready to land the troops.

At this juncture the wind shifted from the east to the south-west, and commenced to blow heavily, so that the ships of war and such transports as had anchored were forced to weigh in all haste and stand out to sea again. Before this untoward occurrence. Colonel Maitland, of the Guards, and Captain Winthorp, of the Royal Navy, were despatched in the *Coburg* cutter, under a flag of truce, to the Dutch admiral. Story, and to Colonel Gilquin, who commanded at the Helder. They were charged with a summons to the two Dutch officers from Lord Duncan, a copy of a declaration made by the Prince of Orange, and a proclamation addressed to the Dutch people by Lieutenant-General Sir Ralph Abercromby.

Of the two last of these documents no notice whatever was taken; but to the first Admiral Story returned, on the 22nd of August, an indignant reply. He declared, that he should consider himself unworthy of Lord Duncan's esteem, and of that of every honest man, were he to accede to the proposal made to him to surrender his fleet, for the service of the Prince of Orange; that he was aware what was his duty to his flag and his country; and that his sentiments would continue the same were the force under Lord Duncan double what it was: at the same time, while winding up with an assurance that, if attacked, he should certainly defend himself, he promised to forward the summons to the Batavian Government. This he did without delay, when the Executive Directory passed a resolution approving of the reply the admiral had made.

Meanwhile, the British fleet continued buffeted about by the winds and waves, until the evening of the 25th, when the weather once more cleared up; so that by the following morning the whole of the ships had again made the land, and anchored in safety off the coast between the villages of Huysduinen and Ketten, just below the Helder Point, this promontory, as before mentioned, forms the northern extremity of the province of North Holland, which is washed by the German Ocean on the west side, and by the inland sea, or rather inundation, called the Zuyder Zee, on the east; whilst on the north it is separated from the Texel Island by a narrow channel, called the Mars Diep, which forms the passage of communication between the German Ocean and the Zuyder Zee.

As soon as the fleet had anchored, orders were issued for the immediate disembarkation of the army, and by three o'clock in the afternoon the transports, with their covering squadron of bombs, sloops, and gun vessels, were in their places, ready to discharge their living freight; the signal for landing was then made, but was countermanded directly after, on account of the lateness of the hour, and the heavy swell which still continued to run from the southward, and occasioned such a surf on the flat beach as would be dangerous to heavily-laden boats. Daylight next morning was then fixed on for a renewal of the attempt to land the army.

In the meantime, the delay in the delay in the arrival of the British expedition had given General Brune ample time to complete his preparations for its reception. On the first appearance of the hostile armament off the coast of North Holland, he at once ordered the concentration in that province of the whole Gallo-Batavian army. The first division of the French army, under General Gouvion, was directed to move to the environs of the city of Haarlem, situated about twelve miles west of Amsterdam; while to the Dutch general, Daendels, was intrusted the important task of opposing the landing of the British. The whole force under the orders of this officer was about 10,000 men; of this corps, one brigade was already cantoned in the peninsula of the Helder, and the remainder came in on the 23rd and 24th of September.

General Daendels then established his headquarters at the little town of Schagenbrug, after confiding to General Van Guericke, who was at the head of about 600 cavalry and 4,000 infantry, the defence of the coast from the Helder down to Groet Keeten. Southward of Groet Keeten, some battalions, under General Van Zuilen Van Nywelt, occupied the villages of Callantsoog, Petten, Campe, and Greet, while the rest of this officer's brigade, except some small detachments left at Haarlem and the city of Alkmaar, formed a second line, extending from Schagen to Bergen.

In this position the Dutch troops remained until the night of the 26th, by which time it became evident to their general that the British would commence to land next morning. He therefore hastily assembled the greater part of his corps, amounting to about 7,000 infantry and cavalry, with field-pieces, and with them took up an advantageous position on the eastern and highest of three ridges of sand-hills, which here stretch along the coast in irregularly-parallel lines from north to south, separated by narrow and tortuous valleys, and themselves intersected by gullies and ravines. The whole of General Van Zuilen's brigade, drawn up between Petten and Callantsoog, formed the left wing of the army; while of General Van Guericke's, two battalions of *chasseurs* were placed among the sand-hills, with a battalion of infantry in support, and two other battalions were formed in line between Groet Keeten and the sea, facing the north.

The remainder of Van Guericke's brigade, comprising three battalions of infantry and two squadrons of cavalry, with four guns, were placed in front of Huysduinen, with their right towards the sea. These dispositions were made by General Daendels, with a view to attacking the British in flank as soon as they should attempt to penetrate into the sand-hills; since he considered that the fire of their covering squadron, would render it impossible to engage them with advantage, as long as they remained on the beach.

The morning, so anxiously expected by both armies, at length began to break, and at three o'clock the first division of the British troops, under Lieutenant-General Sir James Pulteney, consisting of about 2,500 infantry of the 3rd brigade and the reserve, were placed in a flotilla of boats manned by seamen both from the British and Russian men-of-war. The signal was then made, and the whole rowed to the shore, and landed in good order, and without loss: Lieutenant Macdonald, of the grenadier company 25th regiment, was the first man to put foot on shore. A heavy cannonade was kept up during the operation by the British covering flotilla of armed vessels and gun-boats, which had the effect of scouring the beach, but caused no loss to the enemy, who were completely sheltered by the first ridge of sand-hills, distant only a half musket-shot from the sea.

The British troops had scarcely formed up on the beach, before they advanced into the sand-hills; and at about five o'clock the action commenced by a sharp struggle for the possession of a semaphore, or signal station, situated on a low eminence. This building, which was subsequently found of great use in directing the movements of the British covering squadron, was quickly carried by the flank companies of the 3rd brigade,[4] and the battalions of Dutch *chasseurs* placed in front of Klein Keeten were then dislodged in succession from several adjoining eminences, and fell back, resisting gallantly, to Greet Keeten. Directly after— after a vain attempt of the battalion placed in reserve there, to stay the further advance of the British infantry—the whole of

---

4. The following anecdote, illustrative of the gallantry and spirit displayed by the British troops on this occasion, occurs in a journal of the period:—"The Grenadiers of the 29th regiment, finding themselves encumbered with their knapsacks, &c., whilst pursuing the enemy through the heavy sand, threw away both them and their provisions. After the battle, they petitioned to have these necessaries replaced, but, from a strict interpretation of the rules of military discipline, the request could not be granted."

the enemy's centre was forced back upon a battalion of infantry and two squadrons of cavalry, which General Van Guericke had moved up to guard the avenues leading into the marshy plain, extending from behind the sand-hills down to the Zuyder Zee.

At about one o'clock the action became general on both sides; for as fast as they landed from their boats, the British troops pushed forward and came into action by detachments. At this time Lieutenant-General Pulteney, who had greatly distinguished himself, received a wound in the arm, and was forced to leave the field, but his place was ably filled by Major-General Coote. On the other side. General Daendels, at length becoming aware of the mistake he had committed, in trying to maintain so extensive a position, resolved upon a vigorous effort to regain his lost ground, by attacking the British right, composed of the 3rd brigade and reserve, with the two battalions hitherto left between Groet Keeten and the sea, while General Van Guericke was directed to fall simultaneously on their left wing, composed principally of the 1st brigade of Guards, who had formed up among the sand-hills.

This combined movement was rendered impracticable of execution, as far as General Van Guericke was concerned, by the large and deep ditches intervening between his troops and the British position; neither did two battalions, which he had left, without orders, in front of Huysduinen, take any part in the conflict. On the British right, Daendels himself, with the two battalions from Groet Keeten, under Colonel Crass, supported by some troops from General Van Zuilen's brigade, made a determined attack, and at first succeeded in outflanking it. There was not sufficient ground on this side to form more than one battalion in line, which was consequently exposed to the whole force of the enemy; "yet, on the whole," says Sir Ralph Abercromby, in his despatch, "the position, though singular, was not, in our situation, disadvantageous, having neither cavalry nor artillery." Soon, however, the guns of the British covering flotilla carried disorder into the Dutch ranks, and they were beaten back into the sand-hills; the battle then continued with varying success until six in the evening.

At this time the British troops had succeeded in dislodging their opponents from the farthest ridge of the sand-hills, the disembarkation of the whole of their infantry was completed, and their field-pieces, dragged up by seamen through the deep sands, had come into action; so that the Dutch general, feeling that to continue the action longer would he futile, ordered a retreat of his whole force. This was effected in good order, the main body of the army retiring into a low and intersected piece of ground, called the Zuype, about six miles distant, where it took up a new position with its left at Petten on the German Ocean, and its right at Oude Sluys, on the Zuyder Zee, while the two battalions left at Huysduinen first spiked the guns in the batteries along the coast, and then rejoined the army by a circuitous route, so as to avoid being intercepted by the British.

In this well-contested action, which left the British masters of the field, and gained for them a secure footing in Holland, the loss on both sides was heavy. In the Dutch army, 137 officers and men were killed, and 950 wounded. The loss of the British amounted to 54 killed, 376 wounded, and 26 missing (besides 20 men drowned in landing, by the boats conveying them being upset in the heavy surf), and fell principally on the infantry regiments in the reserve, consisting of the 23rd Royal Welsh Fusiliers and the 55th regiment, under Colonel Macdonald, who was himself wounded, though not so severely as to be compelled to relinquish his command, and on the 2nd or Queen's, 27th, 29th, and 85th regiments in the 3rd or Major-General Coote's brigade. The 1st brigade of Guards, under Major-General D'Oyley, sustained some loss, chiefly in the grenadier battalion; but in the 2nd brigade, under Major-General Burrard, the 1st battalion of the Coldstreams only were slightly engaged; and the 4th brigade, under Major-General Moore, did not get into action at all.

Only three officers were slain; but of these, two were field officers, namely, Lieutenant-Colonels Smollet of the 1st Foot Guards, Major-General D'Oyley's Brigade Major, and Hay, Commanding Royal Engineers, whose thigh was shattered by a round shot. On Lieutenant-Colonel Hay's death, the command of the Royal Engineers devolved on Captain Bruyeres, but Lieutenant-Colonel Twiss was sent to take command as soon as news of the fall of the former officer reached England. Among the wounded officers, 23 in number, was Lieutenant-Colonel Graham, who was shot in the left temple by a Dutch rifleman as he was leading his regiment, the 27th, to the charge.[5]

The results of this victory were, for the British, most numerous and important. As soon as the defeat of the Dutch army became known at the Helder, their fleet, which had been at anchor in the Mars Diep, at once got under weigh and retired into the Zuyder Zee, where it took up a new position behind the Texel Island, in a narrow and intricate channel called the Vlieter. Before his departure. Admiral Story received a message from General Daendels, advising him to close the Mars Diep by sinking some old ships in it; but from want of time, this could not be effected. At the same time, the garrison at the Helder Point, consisting of nearly 2,000 men, mostly German troops in Dutch pay, evacuated the fort, after spiking the guns on its batteries and destroying their carriages, and retired with great secrecy through the marshes towards the town of Medemblick.

As it was a paramount object of the British commanders, to obtain possession of this post in order to secure a safe anchorage for their shipping, the 4th brigade, under Major-General Moore, supported by the 2nd brigade, under Major-General Burrard, had been already placed under orders to move against it from Callantsoog at daybreak on the 28th of August. By its evacuation, however, the employment of so large a force by the British general was rendered unnecessary, and the fort was quietly taken possession of at nine o'clock the same evening, by Major-General Moore, with the 2nd battalion 1st Royals and 92nd Highlanders, under Lieutenant-Colonels Lumsdaine and the Marquis of Huntly. In the post were found a number of guns, both for garrison and field service, and all in good condition.

By its capture, the passage to the inner road, called the Nieu-

---

5. For lists of killed and wounded, nominal lists of officers, &;c., see Appendix No. 3.

we Diep, was laid open, and on the morning of the 28th, Captain Winthorp, of the *Circe* frigate, took possession of the Dutch ships of war laid up in ordinary there. These were—the guard ship *Broederschap*, 54 guns; *Unwachten*, 66-gun ship; 44-gun ships, *Hector, Diussee, Expedition, Constitutie, Belle Antoinette,* and *Unie*: frigates, *Helder,* 32; *Venus,* 24; *Alarm,* 24; *Minerva* 24; and *Folloch,* 24: the Indiamen, *Dreighterlahn, Howda,* and *Vreedlust;* and a sheer hulk. The naval arsenal at Nieuwe Werk, containing 95 pieces of artillery, fell into the hands of the British at the same time. By these successes, a reinforcement of 5,000 infantry, consisting of the 1st and 2nd battalions 17th, 1st and 2nd battalion 20th, 1st and 2nd battalion 40th, and the 63rd regiment, which had just arrived from England, under the command of Major-General Don, was enabled to disembark at the Nieuwe Diep, and join the army.

By this accession, the force under the orders of Lieutenant-General Sir Ralph Abercromby was increased to 16,000 effectives. Had the Butch remained in possession of the batteries of the Helder, the newly-arrived regiments would have had to lie outside in their ships, as the stormy weather had now recommenced, and it would have been impossible for them to disembark on the open beach, as the first division had done. The 1st battalion 17th regiment, 686 strong; 2nd battalion 17th, 676; 1st battalion 40th, 684; 2nd battalion 40th, 645, were constituted the 5th brigade of the army, under Major-General Don; the 1st and 2nd battalions 20th regiment, each 774 strong, and the 63rd regiment, 761 strong, the 6th brigade, under Major-General the Earl of Cavan.

Of these four regiments, the 17th had come home in March, 1799, at the evacuation of St. Domingo; the 20th in March, 1796, from Jamaica; the 40th in the spring of 1799, from the Leeward Islands; and the 63rd in May, 1799, from Jamaica. Their ranks were now filled with raw volunteers[6] from the embodied militia—all their old soldiers having perished in the West Indies, or been draughted to weak regiments out there, on their own corps returning home. As an instance of the extent to which this draughting was carried on, it may be mentioned that the 20th, on its return home, could only muster between 60 and 70 non-commissioned officers and men.

After the occupation of the Helder, the reduction of the Dutch fleet now anchored near the Vleiter became the next object to be attained by the British expedition. This fleet was composed of eight ships of the line, three frigates, and a sloop, as follows:—*Washington*, 74, Captain Capelle, flag of Rear-Admiral Story; *Guelderland*, 68, Captain Waldeck; *Admiral de Ruyter*, 68, Captain Huijs; *Utrecht*, 68, Captain Kolf; *Cerberus*, 68, Captain De Zoug; *Leyden*, 68, Captain Van Braam; *Beschermer*, 54, Captain Eilbracht; *Batavier*, 64, Captain Van Senden; *Amphitrite*, 44, Captain Schutter; *Mars*, 44, Captain De Bock; *Ambuscade*, 32, Captain Riverij; *Galathea*, 16, Captain Droop. The accomplishment of this service was intrusted by Lord Duncan to Vice-Admiral Mitchell, who fixed upon the 30th of August to proceed upon the attack, some delay being necessary in order to enable him to collect a sufficient number of pilots at the Helder to take charge of all his ships.

On the morning of that day, at eight o'clock, Lord Duncan himself parted company in the *Kent*, 74, with several of the Russian 74-gun ships, whose draught of water was so great as to preclude all possibility of their being able to get through the Mars Diep, and set sail to join the North Sea fleet at their accustomed anchorage off Aldborough. Three hours before Lord Duncan's departure. Vice-Admiral Mitchell got under weigh with his squadron, consisting of 11 small two-deckers (nine British and two Russian) and five frigates, and stood in towards the Texel with a fair wind. In running into the Mars Diep, two of the former—the 64-gun ship *America*, and the Russian 66-gun ship *Ratwiesan*, with the frigate *Latona*, 38—got on shore; the *Latona* soon after got off and rejoined the admiral, but the two large ships remained stuck fast.

The rest of the squadron passed the Helder Point and Texel in safety, and then continued its course along the Texel until it

6. See Appendix No. 4, for lists of Volunteer given by the Militia to the Line.

entered the channel leading down to the Vleiter. The British line of battle was formed as follows:—*Glatton*, 64, Captain Cobb; *Romney*, 50, Captain Lawford; *Isis* (flag), 60, Captain Oughton; *Veteran*, 64, Captain Dickson; *Ardent*, 64, Captain Bertie; *Belliqueux*, 64, Captain Bulteel; *Monmouth*, 64, Captain Hart; *Overyssel* (late Dutch), 64, Captain Bazeley; and Russian ship *Mistisloff*, 66, Captain Moller; with the frigates *Melpomene*, SS, Captain Sir C. Hamilton; *Shannon*, 32, Captain Pater; *Juno* 32, Captain Dundas; and *Lutine*, 32, Captain Monckton.

At about half-past ten o'clock, when he had approached to within a sufficient distance of the Dutch fleet, Vice-Admiral Mitchell, in pursuance of instructions received from Lord Duncan, dispatched Commander Rennie, of the *Victor* sloop of war, under a flag of truce, with a peremptory summons to the Dutch admiral to hoist the colours of the Prince of Orange immediately, or else take the consequences of a refusal. On his way to the Dutch fleet, Captain Rennie met another flag of truce, with two Dutch captains, whom Vice-Admiral Story had sent on his side to the British commander. With these he at once returned on board the *Isis*, when they requested Admiral Mitchell to anchor, so as to give time for negotiation.

The British squadron accordingly anchored in line at a short distance from the Dutch, and the two envoys were then sent back to their admiral, with injunctions to warn him against altering the position of his ships or injuring them in any way, and to tell him to submit in one hour, or take the consequences. In less than an hour the Dutch captains returned, with a verbal message that their squadron would submit, the officers to be considered as prisoners on parole, until instructions as to the manner in which they were to be disposed of could be received from England or from the Prince of Orange. Soon afterwards, all the ships comprising their squadron hauled down the ensign of the Batavian Republic, and substituted for it the standard of the Prince.

Vice-Admiral Mitchell then issued a short manifesto, calling on their crews to behave peaceably, and also dispatched an

English officer on board each ship to take charge, in accordance with a request made by the Dutch admiral, in a letter addressed by him to Vice-Admiral Mitchell, just before his surrender. In this letter he also declared that he acknowledged no sovereign except the representatives of the Batavian people, and that it was only the misconduct of his crews in refusing to fight that had occasioned his surrender.[7]

This surrender of the Dutch fleet at the Texel was the third great blow which their marine had sustained at the hands of the British fleets in the course of little more than three years; for, on the 17th August, 1796, a squadron, composed of two ships of the line and seven smaller vessels, under Admiral Lucas, had surrendered without resistance to Vice-Admiral Sir George Keith Elphinstone, in Saldanha Bay, Cape of Good Hope; and, on the 11th October, 1797, their North Sea fleet, under Admiral De Winter, had been signally defeated, with the loss of 15 ships, by the British fleet under Duncan, in the glorious Battle of Camperdown. Nevertheless, after these serious losses, there still remained to the Batavian Republic a fleet of 15 sail of the line, stationed at Amsterdam, Flushing, and in the Meuse, together with several 44-gun ships, frigates, and smaller vessels.[8]

The ships captured by Vice-Admiral Mitchell at the Helder and Texel were all sent to England a few days after, escorted by the British ships of war *Glatton*, *Veteran*, *Ardent*, *Belliqueux*, *Monmouth*, and *Overyssel*, and the Russian ship *Mistisloff*. The colours of the prizes and Admiral Story's flag were sent home, in charge of Lieutenant Gibbons, of the *Isis*, to the Lords Commissioners of the Admiralty, by whom they were forwarded to the Prince of Orange, then residing at Hampton Court. After this success, Vice-Admiral Mitchell made arrangements for co-operating on the Zuyder Zee with the army on the shore, while a flotilla of gunboats, calculated to act not only on the coast but on the inland navigation, was fitted out under the direction of Captain Sir Home Popham.

---

7. For correspondence, &c., on this occasion, see Appendix No. 5.
8. For a list of these, see Appendix No. 6.

CHAPTER 2

The Battle of Bergen

Immediately on hearing that the fleet under Admiral Story had surrendered, and that the free navigation of the Zuyder Zee was consequently left open to the British, the Dutch general, Daendels, became alarmed for the safety of the left of his army, behind which he conceived it probable, that Abercromby might attempt to throw a body of troops from his shipping. He therefore fell back the very evening of the surrender of the fleet, towards Alkmaar, and took up a new position between that town, and the village of Avenhorn, in front of the Scheermer, a large lake or inundation. In this situation he considered that his army would be well placed to move rapidly on the line of Purmerend and Monnikendam, towards the shore of the Zuyder Zee, should the British force him to retire further or make any attempt to advance that way on Amsterdam.

On the other hand, Lieutenant-General Sir Ralph Abercromby did at once resolve to profit by his superiority of numbers, and the advantages which recent events afloat had given him, though not exactly in the manner that Daendels anticipated. Since the 27th of August his army had remained on the sandhills, extending in a line from the Helder Point to the village of Callantsoog, a distance of seven miles. In this situation the troops were employed in fortifying themselves with a chain of breastworks and redoubts, and while thus engaged were unfortunately exposed to the severity of the weather; indeed, the only means by which the soldiers could manage to protect themselves against the cold and the frequent showers of rain, was by lying in trenches scooped out of the sandy soil.

The communication with the fleet was also interrupted by the continual storms, so that the supply of provisions had become very irregular and uncertain. On the 1st of September, therefore, an order for an advance into the interior was received with the greatest satisfaction both by officers and men. Leaving the peninsula of the Helder, the army entered the tract of country called the Zuype. This district, formerly a great marsh stretching from one sea to the other, was some centuries back converted by the industry of its inhabitants into a cultivated and fertile plain, intersected by numerous canals.

As usual in Holland, each of these canals is bordered by high dykes, on which many houses are built for safety from inundation. Here the British army took up a new position, its right resting at Petten, on the German Ocean, and its left at Oude Sluys, on the Zuyder Zee; in front it was covered by the Groot Sluys of the Zuype canal, an embankment which afforded peculiarly advantageous positions, as from its great height it commanded a view far down all the avenues of approach. As a further protection for the army against any sudden attack, measures were at once taken for the erection of small redoubts, to be mounted with field-pieces, at intervals along the dyke, which, from the circumstance of its running the whole length of the canal—not in a straight line, but in such a way as to form several circular and angular projections—and also from its having an excellent gravelled road running along the top, was especially adapted for conversion into a line of defence.

The villages on the other side, between Schagen and Krabbendam, were also occupied as advanced posts. By this forward movement a tolerably extensive tract of country was laid open for the troops to forage in, and, before long, a plentiful supply of fresh provisions, chiefly fine black cattle and sheep, was obtained, together with some wagons and teams, which were greatly needed for the transport of the army. Quarters were also obtained for the soldiers, which might be considered luxurious as compared with those they had occupied on the sand-hills; these were numerous large farmhouses, erected in the 16th and 17th centuries, which, having all their offices under one roof, and being surrounded by barns, made excellent and commodious barracks.

In this situation, with his headquarters established in the town of Schagenbrug, Sir Ralph Abercromby determined to remain acting on the defensive until the Russian auxiliary corps, or the powerful reinforcements expected from England under the Duke of York, should arrive. The first instalment of these, being the 11th light dragoons, about 500 strong, arrived at the Helder on the 4th of September, and were at once disembarked, the men swimming their horses to the beach. The transports which had brought them were then ordered to return to the Downs, to bring over further reinforcements of cavalry.

While the British army thus remained in a state of forced inactivity, the enemy to the southward were daily gathering strength. With the exception of a few small detachments left in the principal towns, all the French troops hitherto stationed in the province of Zealand had been directed to move to Haarlem, and the division under General Dumonceau was likewise on its way to North Holland from the eastern provinces. The National Guards were also called out, and formed out into reserves, ready to march on any point that might be threatened; while for the defence of Amsterdam, where the garrison of regular troops had been reduced to a single French battalion, a flotilla of gunboats was organised to act on the Pampus, as the channel leading from the Zuyder Zee to the city is called, and batteries erected on its shore opposite the point of Buykslot.

Having completed these dispositions for the security of the other provinces. General Brune proceeded himself into North Holland, and arrived on the 2nd of September at Alkmaar, just as the rear-guard of General Gouvion's division marched in there. Considering the line occupied by General Daendels was too extensive, he at once caused the evacuation of Avenhorn on the right, and concentrated the Dutch troops between Rustemberg

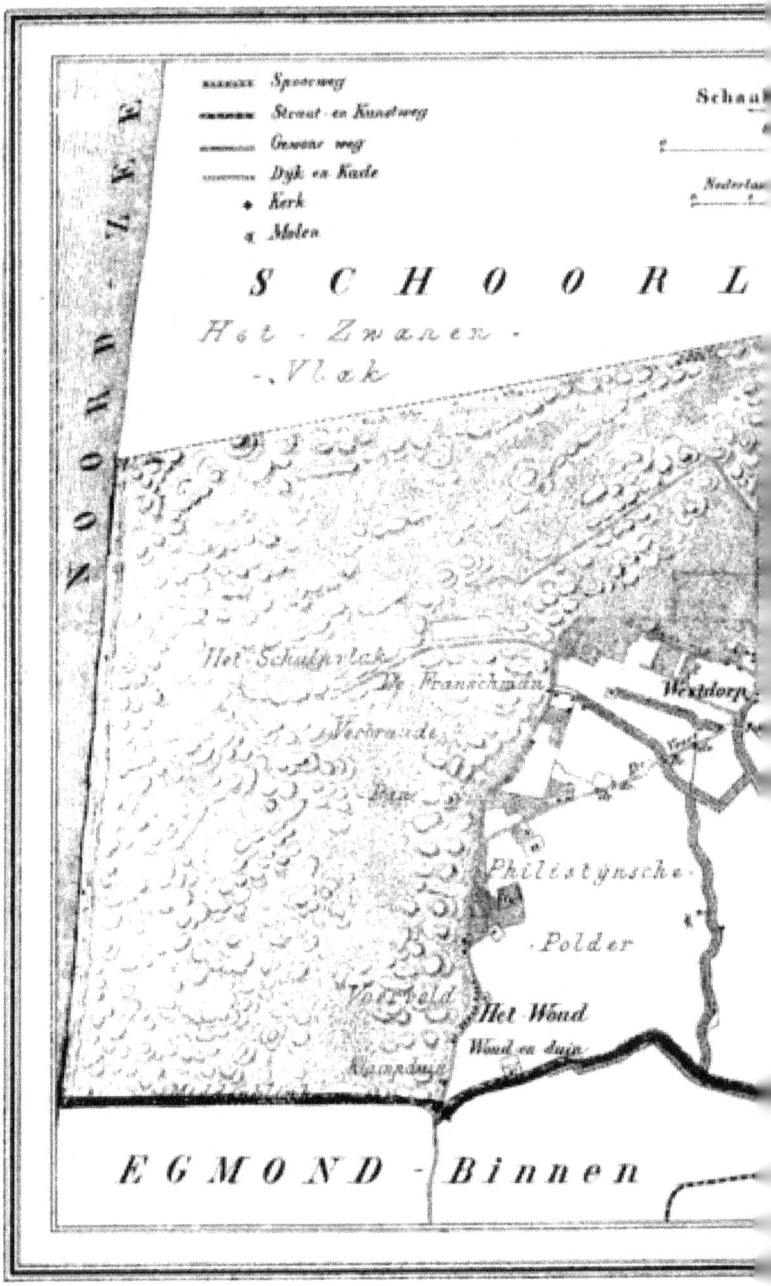

Legend:
- ━━━━━ Spoorweg
- ━━━━━ Straat - en Kunstweg
- ─────── Gewone weg
- ········· Dijk en Kade
- + Kerk
- ¤ Molen

Schaal

Nederlan

NOORDZEE

S C H O O R L

Het - Zwanen -
- . Vlak

Het Schulpvlak

De Franschman

Westdorp

Verbrande

Philistijnsche

. Polder

Het Woud

Woud en duin

E G M O N D - Binnen

and the Koe Dyke, while the French troops, about 7,000, under General Vandamme, were charged with the defence of the interval between Alkmaar and the sea. The advanced posts were established at the villages of Oude-Carspel, Schoreldam, and Schorel; and the headquarters of General Brune, as commander-in-chief of the Gallo-Batavian army, at St. Pancras, a village to the northward of Alkmaar.

In this position the French and Dutch troops remained until the 8th of September; on that day General Dumonceau arrived with a division of Dutch troops, about 6,000 strong, which was placed in the centre at Koe Dyke. By this accession General Brune's army was increased to about 21,000 effectives; and, acting upon peremptory orders received from the Batavian Directory, he now planned a combined attack upon the centre and right of the British position, in the hope of being able to crush the corps of Abercromby before the arrival of the Russians and the Duke of York. The morning of the 10th was fixed on for the attack, to be made by his whole force in three columns.

On the right, a body of Dutch troops, under General Daendels, was to assemble in front of St. Pancras and advance down the Lange Dyke to carry the villages of St. Maarten and Ennigenburg. The centre column, likewise composed entirely of Dutch troops, under General Dumonceau, was to march from Schoreldam against Krabbendam, carry a bridge which there spanned the Zuype Sluys, and so force the head of the British position. To the left column, composed of all the newly-arrived French troops, under General Vandamme, was assigned the difficult task of moving out from Schorel, possessing themselves of the villages of Greet and Campe, and then, after driving the British outposts from the sand-dyke, force their way down the Slaper Dyke, a road skirting the Downs to Petten, so as to turn Abercromby's right, and so, by rendering his present position untenable, compel him to fall back to that which he had occupied on first landing.

At daybreak on the day appointed, the several columns were put in motion; but, fortunately, information of the impending attack had been conveyed to the British general and dispositions made for their reception. On their left, Vandamme's column, after passing through the sand-hills, forced back the British advanced posts, and then attacked the two brigades of British foot-guards, who were appointed to defend the head of the Great Dyke and the Slaper Dyke. Some companies of French grenadiers penetrated as far as the canal bordering on the Great Dyke, but found themselves unable to ford it, and were all either killed or taken. After several ineffectual attempts to storm the position, in one of which General David was slain. General Vandamme found himself taken in flank by the fire of four British armed vessels stationed near the shore, and thereupon fell back along the road to Alkmaar.

The attack of the centre column, under General Dumonceau, on Krabbendam, was not more successful than that of Vandamme on the British right. At the hour appointed for moving, one brigade of Dutch infantry was not forthcoming, and another, tinder General Bonhomme, having by some mistake taken the road to Ennigenbrug, got in the way of the right column, under General Daendels, advancing to attack that post. This disconcerted the whole plan as regarded the Dutch troops, for General Dumonceau, fearing to lose time, took upon himself to send General Bonhomme with part of his brigade against Ennigenburg, whilst he himself led the remainder against Krabbendam.

The village was soon carried, in spite of a heavy fire from some field-pieces placed to enfilade the approaches; but the attempt of the Dutch infantry to storm the strong and commanding position at the head of the dyke of the Zuype canal was foiled by the determined gallantry of the two battalions of the 20th regiment, under Lieutenant-Colonel Smyth and Major Ross. Abercromby himself commanded here, and bringing up some other battalions from the left, he drove the Dutch troops back on Schoreldam, while two French battalions, which had been detached to their support and had just entered the village of Krabbendam, were also compelled to give way.

By this check, General Daendels, who, on finding the road to Ennigenburg obstructed by Dumonceau's brigade, had advanced to St. Maarten's and carried that village, in spite of a spirited defence by Colonel Spencer and the 40th regiment, found himself obliged to give up all idea of making further impression on that side and hasten to General Bonhomme's support. Having succeeded in rallying their disordered troops, the Dutch generals again brought them up to the attack, but with no better success than before; and on seeing his right threatened by the British reserve, who were advancing from Schagen, Daendels fell back at about ten o'clock to St. Pancras. From this village they decamped, on a false alarm that the British were pursuing them, a few hours later. The loss in the Gallo-Batavian army was supposed to be nearly 1,000, including 40 officers killed and wounded. In the British army the loss was comparatively slight, amounting to only 37 men killed, 14 officers and 133 men wounded, and 18 men missing. Among the wounded officers was Lieutenant-Colonel Smyth of the 20th, shot through the leg, and Major-General Moore, who commanded on the right, received a slight flesh-wound.[9]

After this engagement, the hostile armies remained for a few days in the positions they had previously occupied, and no further offensive operations were undertaken on either side. Abercromby, on his part, held to his former determination of remaining on the defensive until the Duke of York should arrive; while General Brune, convinced, by the result of the action of the 10th, that any further attempt to dislodge the British from their entrenchments, or to oppose the landing of their other divisions, would he futile, contented himself by taking measures to render his position as strong as possible, in order to resist their penetrating farther into the country; for this purpose he caused the roads to be cut up, redoubts constructed at the heads of the different dykes, and the natural difficulties already in existence increased as much as possible.

---

9. For lists of killed and wounded, nominal list of officers wounded, &,c.. see Appendix No. 7.

During this tacit suspension of hostilities, the expected powerful reinforcements for the British army arrived. During the 12th (September, and on the following morning, the first division of the Russian contingent, consisting of eight battalions of infantry, about 7000 effectives, under the command of Lieutenant-General D'Hermann, arrived at the Helder from Revel, and were at once disembarked and marched down to strengthen the right of the position on the Zuype. On the evening of the 13th, His Royal Highness the Duke of York and Lieutenant-General Dundas also landed at the Helder from the *Amethyst* frigate, having sailed from the Downs on the 9th. They were followed by the third and last division of British troops, consisting of eleven battalions of infantry, one regiment of cavalry (the 7th Light Dragoons), and a body of artillery. The 7th Light Dragoons had embarked at Ramsgate; the infantry at Deal, to which place they marched from the camp on Barham Downs. After disembarking at the Helder, these troops marched up to Schagenburg, where the men were quartered in the churches and the officers billeted on the private houses. The newly-arrived regiments were brigaded as follows:—

7th Brigade, under Major-General the Earl of Chatham: The 1st, 2nd, and 3rd battalions 4th King's Own, and the 31st regiment.

8th Brigade, under Major-General His Royal Highness Prince William of Gloucester: The 1st battalion 5th regiment, 686 strong; 2nd battalion 5th, 666; 1st battalion 35th regiment, 607; and 2nd battalion 35th, 614.

9th Brigade, under Major-General Manners: The 1st and 2nd battalions 9th regiment and the 56th regiment, the latter 676 strong.

Of the above regiments, the 4th and 5th had both come home from Canada in 1797; the 9th from Grenada in the autumn, and the 31st from Barbadoes in July of the same year, and the 56th from St. Domingo in January, 1799; the 35th alone had been some time on home service. The 9th regiment, having received

2,695 volunteers from the Gloucester and other militia corps in the vicinity of London, had been formed, liked the 4th, into three battalions, but, unlike that regiment, it only brought two of them into the field. The 31st had obtained 955 volunteers from the militia, but as it had come home from Barbadoes only 85 strong, this number was merely sufficient to complete it to the strength of a single battalion.

Two flank battalions, one of ten companies of grenadiers under Lieutenant-Colonel Baylis, 35th regiment, and the other of the same number of light infantry under Lieutenant-Colonel Shairpe, 9th regiment, had been formed from the flank companies of the 4th, 5th, 9th, 31st, and 35th regiments before leaving Barham Downs, and were now ordered to be attached to the reserve, under Colonel Macdonald. To Lieutenant-Colonel Lord Paget, of the 7th Light Dragoons, was given the command of the cavalry brigade, formed of his own regiment, the 11th Light Dragoons, under Lieutenant-Colonel Childers, and two squadrons 18th Light Dragoons, under Lieutenant-Colonel Stewart, in all about 1,200 sabres.

At the Helder, before proceeding to join Sir Ralph Abercromby at Schagenbrug, the Duke of York had an interview with the Hereditary Prince of Orange, who had arrived at the Texel the 8th of September, and thence come on to the former place, after a vain attempt to effect a diversion in favour of the British army. Landing in the province of Overyssel, he had put himself at the head of a force of 1000 men, collected for him at Lingen by officers formerly in his service; he then marched against Coevorden, and on the 3rd of September summoned that fortress to surrender. The summons was treated with contempt by the Republican governor, and on a party of National Guards moving against him from Arnheim, the Prince was compelled to dismiss his followers and take shipping at Embden for the Helder.

Here he was at present occupied in organizing into regiments a number of volunteers from the crews of the captured Dutch fleet, and some deserters who had come over from the Batavian army since the action on the sand-hills. The British 69th regiment, detached from the 3rd brigade, was also encamped outside the Helder, and remained there as a rear-guard during the whole campaign.

On the arrival of the Duke of York at Schagenbrug, his first measure was to considerably extend the position of his army, a measure rendered absolutely necessary by the arrival of the British and Russian reinforcements. In this new disposition, the Russians, whose second division, under Major d'Essen, had also arrived, formed the right wing of the army; while, on the left, the 4th brigade, under Major-General Moore, was pushed forward to Colhorn. By the 15th of September the total strength of the forces under the Duke's command was about 33,000 effectives, in 46 battalions and 10 squadrons, with a numerous train of artillery; but the disembarkation of the last arrivals was carried on so leisurely, that the whole were not assembled on the line of the Zuype before the 18th.

The Duke of York then determined to avail himself of his great numerical superiority of force to undertake a general offensive movement against the whole of the enemy's position in front of Alkmaar, and, by turning their flank, force them to retire to the southward. The season was advanced, and contrary winds and the other obstacles to the speedy assembly of the several divisions composing his army, had enabled the enemy to collect the means of opposition from several quarters. Strong reinforcements, sent up by the French Directory, were rapidly advancing between the Meuse and Rhine Rivers, and the news of their approach had considerably damped whatever disposition might have existed among the Dutch people to favour the cause of the Prince of Orange; while in Switzerland, the operations of the allied armies had taken a turn, which forbade any expectation that they would serve as a useful diversion to the attempt in Holland.

By an advance into the country, therefore, the British commander-in-chief designed to obtain a more defensible position, and to lay open a more extensive and fertile tract of country for the subsistence of his army. That the former object would be readily obtained by moving to the southward will be easily understood when it is stated that the peninsular of Holland increases in breadth to the extent of 36 miles at Camperdown, and then, a few miles below, narrows again, so that at Shaerdam, two miles beyond the city of Hoorn, it is only 16 miles across. Posted at Shaerdam, therefore, the British army would have but a comparatively small line to defend, with a large and fertile tract of country in its rear in which to forage; its left flank would be protected by the Zuyder Zee, and its right by the German Ocean, while the centre would be admirably covered by the large fortified town of Alkmaar, and the whole position further strengthened by the broad canals and their high and strongly-constructed dykes or embankments, running in parallel lines across the country.

The position from which the Duke of York had it in contemplation to drive the enemy had by this time been rendered by them one of no ordinary strength. Their left wing, composed entirely of French troops under General Vandamme, was strongly posted on the first ridge of the lofty sand-hills, known as the heights of Camperduyn; these heights rise abruptly from the plain in front of Petten to an altitude of about 300 feet, and stretch away in a south-easterly direction towards Alkmaar, presenting a steep and thickly-wooded face to the interior of the country, but, on the other side, sloping away gradually from their summit down to the sea coast. From the village of Campe, situated in front of these heights, which was itself strongly entrenched and guarded, a large canal, which branches off from the Groot Sluys of the Zuype canal at Krabbendam, runs along the foot of the heights all the way down to Alkmaar.

The enemy's right, composed wholly of Dutch troops under General Daendels, lay in the plain in front of Alkmaar, covered by strong redoubts erected at Oude-Carspel, a village situated at the head of the Lange Dyke, as the principal road leading to the first-named place is called. Two other fortified posts had been established at the villages of Warmanhuysen and Schoreldam, situated, the first, on the plain in front of their centre, and the latter behind it, at the head of the Koe Dyke, and rather nearer to the sand-hills. Moreover, the whole plain in front of their line of posts was intersected at every 300 or 400 yards by broad and deep canals and large ditches, running out of the main canal from Krabbendam to Alkmaar, but having no other communication with one another; and, to increase the natural difficulties of an approach to the fortified villages, the bridges on the only two or three roads leading to them had been broken down, and abattis laid down at certain intervals on the roads themselves.

Strong as was this position of the Gallo-Batavian army in front and on the left flank, it was still very defective in one very material point, for General Brune had committed the error of leaving his right totally uncovered, although on that side the country was naturally very strong. The Duke of York, therefore, determined to send a strong corps to turn the enemy's position before they should find out their mistake and occupy this strong country—from which, were it once in their possession, it would be extremely difficult to force them—and at the same time to assail them in front with the rest of his army.

To execute the first part of the plan, Lieutenant-General Sir Ralph Abercromby advanced from Colhorn at 6 o'clock on the evening of the 18th of September, at the head of a column of 9,000 men. This column, consisting of two squadrons of the 18th light dragoons, the 4th, 6th, and 7th brigades, under Major-Generals Moore and the Earls of Cavan and Chatham, and the reserve under Colonel Macdonald, was intended to arrive next morning at the city of Hoorn and then push on to Purmerend; thence, should the attack on the enemy's left succeed, to march direct on Amsterdam.

The remainder of the British and Russian troops were under arms and in motion at an hour before daybreak on the 19th of September. They were formed in three principal columns, commanded respectively by Lieutenant-Generals D'Hermann, Dundas, and Sir James Pulteney. Of these, the first, under Lieutenant-General D'Hermann, consisting of twelve battalions of

Russian infantry under Lieutenant-General Jereptoff and Major-Generals Essen and Schutorff; the 10th British brigade, under Major-General Manners; and the 7th Light Dragoons, under Lieutenant-Colonel Lord Paget—between 7,000 and 8,000 in all—was to advance on the right from Petten, along the Sand Dyke and the Slaper Dyke, against the villages of Campe and Groete, and then take the roads leading thence to Bergen and Egmont-op-Zee—the one passing through Schorel, and the other along the heights of Camperduyn.

By this movement it was expected that the small body of French troops stationed at Egmont-op-Zee would be forced to retire, so that General Bruno's left flank would be laid open, and the rest of Vandamme's corps being dislodged at the same time from their position on the Camperduyn heights and the villages below, Lieutenant-General D'Hermann would be able to take possession of Bergen, a considerable village situated on the property of the Prince of Nassau, four miles north-west of Alkmaar. The second, or centre column, under Lieutenant-General Dundas, consisted of a wing of the 11th Light Dragoons, the brigades of British foot-guards under Major-Generals D'Oyley and Burrard, and the 8th brigade, under Prince William of Gloucester—about 5,000 in all. This column, to which both the Duke of York and the Hereditary Prince of Orange attached themselves, was more particularly intended to support that under Lieutenant-General D'Hermann, by forcing in succession the posts established by the enemy in the villages of Warmanhuysen and Schoreldam, and then moving on in conjunction with it towards Bergen.

In the attack on the two fortified villages it was to be assisted by three Russian battalions—about 2,000 bayonets—who were to advance from Krabbendam under Major-General Sedmoratzky, and by three gunboats, each carrying a 12-pound carronade and manned by seamen under the direction of Sir Home Popham and Captain Godfrey, of the Royal Navy, which had succeeded in penetrating into the Alkmaar canal. The third, or left column, under Lieutenant-General Sir James Pulteney, consisting of the other wing of the 11th Light Dragoons and the 3rd and 5th brigades under Major-Generals Coote and Don—in all 5,000 men—was to advance down the Lange Dyke against Oude-Carspel; but as that important post was strongly entrenched, it was intended that this division should not attack seriously, but rather confine itself to demonstrations, so as to prevent General Daendels from sending troops to the support of the French troops on his left. Should he, however, succeed, by any fortunate chance, in gaining possession of Oude-Carspel, Sir James Pulteney was to co-operate with Dundas in the direction of Schoreldam, and detach strong parties to his left, between Alkmaar and Haarlem, to open a communication with the column under Lieutenant-General Sir Ralph Abercromby.

The original intention was that the three columns of the right should advance simultaneously, but, owing to some mistake, for which the allied generals afterwards mutually blamed another, the attack was commenced by the Russians on the right two hours before the appointed time. Quitting his position at Petten at three o'clock in the morning, Lieutenant-General D'Hermann passed over the canal and led his troops against some works constructed by the enemy at the extremity of the Slaper Dyke. The Russian infantry advanced to the attack with such spirit and gallantry that this post and the villages of Groet and Campe were rapidly carried, and their defenders forced to give way and retire in confusion over the open downs towards Bergen, after several vain attempts to reform under cover of the sand-hills. Elated at this success, the Russian column rapidly pursued in two divisions—the one led by Lieutenant-General D'Hermann along the road to Schorel, and the other, under Lieutenant-General Jereptoff, over the sand-hills.

As the former approached Schorel, a murderous fire was opened on the flank of his column by some of the fugitives from behind the adjacent hedges and ditches. On perceiving this, Major-General Manners—who, it was intended, should have remained in reserve behind the Russians—proceeded to dislodge them, and in so doing lost his way, and followed a body of the enemy down the road towards Schoreldam with his whole brigade.

On arriving in front of Schorel, the Russian column, led by Lieutenant-General D'Hermann, encountered three French battalions, whom General-of-Brigade Rostolan, chief of the Gallo-Batavian staff, had succeeded in rallying, and had drawn up in line between the sand-hills and Schoreldam, with their light field-pieces so placed as to sweep all the approaches. These the Russians at once attacked, and an obstinate engagement was then sustained for three hours with no advantage to either side. At the end of that time, General Rostolan, over-hearing that the other Russian column was descending from the sand-hills to take him in flank, and that the British had now commenced the attack of Schoreldam, became alarmed lest he should be cut off from Bergen, and fell back precipitately to that village.

The Russians followed so closely in pursuit, that Rostolan, although reinforced there by five battalions under General Gouvion, was unable to complete his dispositions for defence before the column under D'Hermann had entered the wooded tract of country which skirts the sand-hills and surrounds Bergen, while that under Lieutenant-General Jereptoff appeared moving down from the heights to attack his left. The French commanders, therefore, retired to some distance beyond the village to await reinforcements; and, in the meantime, busied themselves in re-forming their broken battalions under cover of the woods.

On entering Bergen, consequently, the Russians found the place totally abandoned, and this circumstance causing them to suppose that no further resistance would be attempted, and that their work for the day was over, they at once piled their arms, and gave themselves up to plundering the village. The opportunity for retrieving the fortune of the day afforded him by this unmilitary conduct, on their part, was promptly seized by General Brune. The obstinate resistance of the brigade under Rostolan, at Schorel, had given him time to bring up some fresh battalions hitherto held in reserve at Alkmaar, and he now reinforced his left with a portion of General Dumonceau's Dutch division, which passed the canal leading from Alkmaar to the Zuype by means of a bridge of communication erected some days before.

On the arrival of these troops near Bergen and the sand-hills, General Vandamme's division became sufficiently strong to resume the offensive. Reserving to himself the direction of the centre, that general at once ordered Gouvion to lead his brigade round the place in the direction of Alkmaar, and sent General Rostolan with two battalions into the woods bordering the sand-hills on his left, charging him to remain there until the combat should be at its height. These arrangements completed, a furious attack was commenced on the Russians, who were taken at a great disadvantage, as several of their battalions were scattered about the adjacent woods, which, with the roads and avenues intersecting them, form a complete maze, while a great number of the soldiers were collecting their plunder in the ruined church.

Although so much scattered, they resisted gallantly, momentarily expecting that succour would arrive from the English, and contested every inch of ground. The French, however, succeeded in penetrating into the village under a heavy fire, and, at last General Vandamme seized a favourable opportunity to charge with four battalions at the point of the bayonet. Unable to withstand the shock, the Russians gave way, and went off, some into the sand-hills, and others towards Schorel. The former were intercepted by the two battalions under General Rostolan, whose sudden and unexpected appearance created a panic among them, and they were then forced back into the village. Here, although broken and dispersed, they continued to defend themselves in the church and houses until all had been killed, wounded, and taken. Among the prisoners were Lieutenant-Generals D'Hermann and Jereptoff, the latter mortally wounded. The other section of the Russian column, under Major-General Essen, retired, hotly pursued by the French, all the way to the village of Schorel.

Meanwhile, Lieutenant-General Dundas, after detaching the

grenadier battalion of the Guards to observe Schoreldam, and placing the 8th brigade, under Major-General Prince William of Gloucester, in reserve between St. Maarten's and Ennigenbrug, had, with the remainder of the second or right column, attacked at daylight the village of Warmanhuysen. This post was soon carried, the 3rd battalion 1st Guards entering on the right, while, on the left, it was gallantly stormed by the Russian brigade from Krabbendam, under Major-General Sedmoratzky.

The 1st battalion 3rd Foot-Guards, and the 2nd battalion 5th regiment, were then detached to open a communication to the left with Lieutenant-General Sir James Pulteney's column, while the rest of the column, strengthened by the 1st battalion 5th regiment, moved on to Schoreldam. The Dutch troops in that village, finding themselves placed between the troops under Dundas and the 9th brigade under Major-General Manners, now advancing from the side of Schorel, soon gave way, and fell back to the Koe Dyke, their general, Dumonceau, having been desperately wounded; two entire battalions, and some companies of grenadiers, which he had despatched towards Schoreldam to cover General Rostolan's retreat, thus found themselves between two fires, and were forced to lay down their arms.

At this juncture, the body of fugitive Russians from Bergen appeared outside of Schorel, the French following close behind them; and after one last effort to make a stand, the former were driven pell-mell into and out of the village. The enemy were then checked, however, by the 9th brigade, consisting of the 1st and 2nd battalions 9th regiment and the 56th regiment, under Major-General Manners, which advanced by the road from Schoreldam, in the teeth of a heavy fire, and retook the village. This brigade was in its turn forced to retreat, closely pursued by the enemy, until they were joined by the 1st battalion 35th regiment, about 600 strong, under Prince William of Gloucester, this single battalion being the only one in his brigade which had not been detached.

Finding that the command in this quarter had devolved upon himself, by the capture of the Russian lieutenant-generals,

Prince William determined to attempt the recapture of Schorel. By staying the onward progress of the enemy with the 35th for a few moments, he gave time for Major-General Manners' brigade to form up in his rear, and then, pushing forward with this support, he succeeded in carrying the village, and the wood skirting it. Directly afterwards, the Duke of York brought up the 1st brigade of Guards, under Major-General D'Oyley, and two Russian battalions of Major-General Sedmoratzky's brigade, from Warmanhuysen; and the whole then pursued the enemy up the sand-hills, and forced them to retire on Bergen. By this time, however, the Russian troops under Major-General Essen, who had expended all their ammunition, and could not, therefore, he induced to renew the combat, had sought shelter behind the entrenchments of the Zuype; the rest of the British and Russian infantry were also exhausted by the fatigues they had undergone, so that the Duke of York was led to give orders for a retreat towards Petten and Zuype Sluys.

This was effected in good order: all the guns, ammunition, waggons, and wounded, being brought off in the face of the enemy. By this retrograde movement of the right wing, the position of the portion of Lieutenant-General Dundas's column, which continued to hold Schoreldam, with the assistance of Sir Home Popham's gunboats, under a well-directed and galling fire from the Dutch artillery, was rendered no longer tenable, and the regiments composing it were forced to fall back to their former position at Krabbendam.

Whilst the right and centre columns continued hotly engaged, the third or left column, under Lieutenant-General Sir James Pulteney, had proceeded to the attack of the fortified post established by the enemy at Oude-Carspel. This place—the first of some straggling villages extending for a distance of from three to four miles down the Lange Dyke, and almost to the outskirts of Alkmaar—was defended by the main body of the Dutch troops, under General Daendels, and no pains had been spared to render it as strong as possible. At the northern extremity of the village, several redoubts and batteries had been constructed and armed with field-pieces, while the place was completely surrounded by deep canals and high dykes. Nevertheless, the dispositions for the attack were soon completed by the British general.

The 3rd brigade, under Major-General Coote, was ordered to advance from Nieudorp Verlaat and attack the enemy's right flank so as to take their position in reverse, while the 5th brigade, under Major-General Don, was to assail their left and centre; two squadrons of the 11th Light Dragoons remained in reserve. Every preparation completed, the 1st and 2nd battalions 40th regiment were led forward by Colonel Spencer, until they arrived behind a dyke parallel to the front of the Dutch lines; the 1st and 2nd battalions 17th followed close in support They were here exposed to a heavy discharge of grape and round shot, shells, and musketry, which brought them to a stand behind an angle of the embankment. Supposing that his assailants had been forced to retire, the Dutch general at once sent out some companies of grenadiers from behind their fortifications, to follow up the supposed advantage. He was speedily undeceived, for the 40th met this detachment with a heavy volley, and then, charging with the bayonet, forced them to fly, and, following close behind, entered the works along with the fugitives.

On the other side, the greater portion of the 3rd brigade had been debarred from taking a share in the assault, by finding that the bridge which formerly spanned a wide and deep canal in front of the enemy's entrenchments had been broken down, and a few companies only of the 2nd, or Queen's, and 29th regiments found means to cross over in canoes, and entered the post at the same time as the 40th and 17th regiments. A thousand Dutch soldiers, who had been intended to oppose Coote's brigade, thus found themselves hemmed in between the two attacking columns, and at once threw down their arms; the remainder, under General Daendels, fled in confusion towards St. Pancras and Alkmaar, galled in their retreat by the fire of the British artillery; and the whole of this important post, with the guns mounted on its works, remained in the possession of Sir

James Pulteney.

It is but just to General Daendels to state that his division had been considerably weakened by a detachment sent to the support of the centre of their army, under General Dumonceau, and that much confusion had been caused in its ranks by the accidental explosion of a tumbril.

This brilliant success was not achieved without considerable loss to the British—the two battalions of the 40th regiment losing 12 officers and 141 men, and the two of the 17th 8 officers and 66 men killed, wounded, and taken—and his ill success on the right rendered it impossible for the Duke of York to profit by it. He was therefore forced to send an order to Sir James Pulteney, who had pushed on to within a short distance of Alkmaar, to withdraw along the Lange Dyke to his old ground. Pulteney reluctantly obeyed; and General Daendels thereupon rallied his troops and reoccupied the village of Broek and others on that road, together with all the batteries that had fallen into the hands of the British when they forced his position at Oude-Carspel.

On the same account, it was deemed necessary to recall the column under Lieutenant-General Sir Ralph Abercromby. That officer had been enabled to move on, without opposition, to the city of Hoorn, the enemy, strange as it may appear, having made no arrangements to guard the approach to Amsterdam on that side. Hoorn, being well affected to the House of Orange, at once opened its gates; and the inhabitants hoisted the Orange flag on the steeples, put Orange cockades in their hats, and received the troops with every possible demonstration of satisfaction. The garrison, consisting of only two companies of Dutch infantry, were made prisoners. From Hoorn it had been intended that Abercromby should push on to Purmerend; and the capture of Oude-Carspel by Pulteney had left the way open to him, by cutting General Daendels off from a retreat thither. The bad state of the roads, and the fatigued state of his troops, however, decided him to remain for the present at Hoorn, and during the night news of the misfortune at Bergen arrived.

THE BATTLE OF BERGEN

A retreat was then ordered, and at once commenced; but before the troops had left Hoorn half an hour, the rain came down in torrents, and converted the road into a mass of mud. Through this the troops struggled on, lighted by the flames of burning villages, until, at an early hour next morning, they regained their former position at Colhorn.

Thus terminates the story of the Battle of Bergen, in which, after thirteen hours and a half of incessant fighting, no results whatever were obtained—and this owing to the misconduct of the Russian corps on the right. By their defeat at Bergen it was that the success of the other three columns was rendered useless, and that the British troops, after overcoming every obstacle opposed by nature and art, were forced to abandon the positions they had won with such gallantry and at so great a loss, and fall back to the very entrenchments from which they had marched in the morning.

When it is considered that General Brune was at the head of at least 13,000 French and 15,000 Dutch troops, and that on the other hand the British and Russian troops engaged were not more than 20,000—since the whole of Abercromby's column did not see a shot fired, and a whole British brigade of infantry and the cavalry were either unable to get into action or else left in rapport—it will be admitted that the English army had no reason to be ashamed of the ultimate failure which attended the operations of the day.

The loss of the Gallo-Batavian army in the Battle of Bergen amounted to about 2,000 of all ranks killed and wounded, and 60 officers and 3,000 non-commissioned officers and men made prisoners by the Russians, between Schorel and Schoreldam, and at Oude-Carspel and Hoorn. Sixteen pieces of artillery and a large supply of ammunition, which the breaking down of the bridges prevented the British troops from bringing off, were also destroyed. The loss of the British and Russian troops was nearly as severe; of the former nearly 1,600, including 49 officers, and of the latter 3,000, were killed, wounded, and missing. Twenty-six field-pieces, being nearly all the artillery they had brought into the field, and seven standards, were also lost by the Russians, and their second in command, Lieutenant-General Jereptoff, who, as well as Lieutenant-General D'Hermann, was made prisoner in Bergen, died of his wounds next day. The officer of highest rank killed in the British army was Lieutenant-Colonel Morris, of the Coldstream Guards.[1]

Two days after the Battle of Bergen, operations were commenced in earnest afloat for the reduction of the various towns situated on the Zuyder Zee. Having shifted his flag into the 20-gun ship *Babet*, Rear-Admiral Mitchell proceeded into this inland sea on the morning of the 21st of September, accompanied by four bomb vessels, brigs *L'Espiègle* and *Speedwell*, *Lady Ann* lugger, and armed ship *Prince William*, with a number of large *schuyts*, to man which, all the available seamen and marines had been draughted from the *Isis* and the frigates *Melpomene* and *Juno*, then lying at the Helder. Approaching Medemblick, which town had already made its submission. Vice-Admiral Mitchell was there joined at noon by the *Dart* sloop of war and two gun-brigs; with these he proceeded on to Enkhausen, and anchored off that town with the whole squadron at three in the afternoon.

A boat, with four men wearing Orange cockades, then came off from the shore, by whose invitation Vice-Admiral Mitchell went on shore with the captains, and was received by the inhabitants with every demonstration of satisfaction. He then went to the *Stadthouse*, and proceeded, pending instructions from the Hereditary Prince of Orange, to reinstate those old and faithful burgomasters who had never taken the oath of allegiance to the Batavian Republic. At the same time he summoned before him, and dissolved the Municipality, amidst the acclamations of the inhabitants, a party of whom lost no time in cutting down the "tree of liberty."

Enkhausen having submitted, Vice-Admiral Mitchell sent Captain Boorder, in *L'Espiègle*, to Steveren, to bring intelligence

1. For lists of killed, wounded, and missing, nominal lists of officers, &c., see Appendix No. 8.

of the disposition of the inhabitants; and on the morning of the 23rd this officer returned, with the information that the people there had hoisted Orange colours, as well as in several neighbouring towns, the inhabitants of all joyfully complying with the same terms as Enkhausen and Medemblick. Captain Boorder, in *L'Espiègle*, with the *Speedwell* under his orders, was then sent to scour the coast between Steveren and Lemmer, and the *Dart*, with two gun-brigs, to cut off the communication between Amsterdam and such towns in East Friesland as had not yet returned to their allegiance.

On the appearance of the British vessels before Lemmer, the garrison of the place rejected the summons to surrender, and placed guns on the pier-head, with a determination to resist. After overcoming the difficulties presented by the shoal water, the *Wolverine*, Captain Bolton, and some other armed vessels, succeeded in bringing their broadsides to bear on the place, and soon drove the enemy from their guns; when a body of seamen and marines disembarked, and took possession of the town without further opposition. After these rapid successes the flotilla coasted onwards to the entrance of the Pampus (the channel leading out of the Wye to Amsterdam), and there captured four gunboats, being a portion of the flotilla intended for the defence of the capital by water.

CHAPTER 3

The Battle of Alkmaar

After the battle of the 19th of September, the possibility of either army recommencing offensive operations was precluded, for some days, by severe and incessant storms, with heavy rains, which had the effect of rendering the roads impassable and laying the fields under water. During this interval of forced repose, some considerable reinforcements arrived at the Helder and joined the British army, which was thus augmented to nearly 40,000 effectives. The principal of these reinforcements was the third division of the Russian contingent—about 6,000 strong—under Major-General Emmé, who landed on the morning of the 26th of September. About 2,000 of this division were encamped between the Nieuve Diep and the Helder, and the rest marched down to Petten, and joined the corps under Major-General Essen, which was thus raised to about the strength it had been before the action of the 19th.

The remainder of the reinforcements comprised several detachments of the different British infantry regiments serving in the field, which had either not been in readiness to embark with their head-quarters, or had been forced by stormy weather to put back to the Channel, or into some neutral port. The cavalry brigade also received a seasonable addition on the 25th of September, by the arrival in transports, from Ramsgate, of three troops of the 15th Light Dragoons, under Lieutenant-Colonel Erskine; and the *Camilla* frigate came in a day or two after from Cowes with the rifle company of the 6th battalion 60th (or

Royal American) regiment, which was then being formed of German and other foreign recruits at Albany Barracks, near Newport, Isle of Wight.

On their side, the Gallo-Batavian generals failed not to take advantage of this suspension of hostilities, to strengthen their advanced posts as much as possible. These were nearly identical with those held by them before the action of the 19th, as, indeed, was their whole position. Their left wing, composed of the French troops under General Vandamme, still held the heights of Camperduyn, and extended towards Bergen, through the villages of Campe, Groete, and Schorel. In the centre, the advanced post of Schoreldam and the Koe Dyke were occupied by a strong body of Dutch troops, under General Dumonceau; while the right wing, also composed of Dutch troops, under General Daendels, were posted in and about Oude-Carspel and the Lange Dyke, for the protection of which several additional works had been constructed.

General Brune had also taken measures to cover his right, and prevent the British from again passing between it and the Zuyder Zee, by inundating the Polders of Scheermer, Beemster, and Purmer, and strongly fortifying the only passages across them—the Dykes of Monnikendam and Purmerend. By this means, the wide space between Alkmaar and the Zuyder Zee was rendered easy of defence by a very small force, and Amsterdam covered on the land side. For its defence by water, a flotilla of sixty gunboats had been brought round from Dunkirk, by the inland navigation, and placed in the Pampus.

Finding that the enemy's right was rendered no longer assailable by reason of the inundations, and deeming that, in fronts their position was now too strong to be attacked with chance of success, the Duke of York now determined to operate with the main body of his army against their left, on the German Ocean, in hopes of being able to make such an impression there as might compel them to retire to the southward. The season was now advancing; the enemy had just been strengthened by the arrival of four battalions of French infantry, and four squadrons of cavalry, and of some newly-raised Dutch battalions, and other reinforcements were daily expected; so that it became an object of the utmost importance to the British commander-in-chief to move against them as soon as possible.

On the 24th of September, he had relieved the British reserve under Colonel Macdonald—which had, up to this time, occupied the advanced posts on the left of the army—by a detachment of 150 of the 18th Light Dragoons, under Lieutenant-Colonel Stewart, and the 8th Infantry brigade, under Prince William of Gloucester, who established his headquarters at the village of Winckel, with his left to the Zuyder Zee and his right at Riendorper Verlaat.[2] Other preparations for the intended advance were made; and, on the 29th of September, when the violence of the weather had in some degree abated, the whole of the British and Russian troops got under arms before dawn, and, on the first appearance of daylight, were put in motion towards the enemy's position.

Before long, however, it was found impossible to proceed, as the roads, from having no hard bottom, were in such a state, that the infantry marched almost knee-deep in mud, while the wide sandy beach, on the right, was rendered equally impassable, by a high tide, with heavy surf, breaking upon it. All idea of bringing on an engagement had, therefore, to be abandoned, and the several brigades fell back to the posts they had marched from.

At length, on the 1st of October, the heavy rains ceased entirely, and the roads were once more rendered practicable for troops by the wind shifting to a drier quarter; several material changes in the disposition of the troops were then carried into effect, preparatory to another general advance against the enemy's position. Those brigades which had, up to this time, formed the left wing, took ground considerably to their right; while those before stationed on the right, inclined towards the centre, to make room for them. Next morning, at six o'clock, the whole army was again under arms, formed, as on the 19th of September, in four columns; but the disposition of these was

---

2. *Military Calendar*, vol. 1.

very materially different from what it had been on that day, for the Russians were now placed in the centre, with British troops on both flanks.

No less than three columns—in the whole about 23,000 men—were assigned for the attack of the French corps in and around Bergen, forming the left wing of the Gallo-Batavian army. Of these, the right column, under Lieutenant-General Sir Ralph Abercromby, was formed of the 1st brigade of guards, and the 4th and 6th brigades, under Major-Generals D'Oyley, Moore, and Hutchinson (the latter commanding in the absence of Lord Gavan, disabled by a fall from his horse); the reserve, under Colonel Macdonald; the 7th, three squadrons of the 11th, and one and a half of the 15th Light Dragoons, under Colonel Lord Paget; details of foot artillery, under Lieutenant-Colonel Whitworth; and one troop of horse artillery, under Major Judson.[3]

These troops—about 8,000 infantry, and between 800 or 900 cavalry, in fourteen battalions and eight and a half squadrons, with twenty field-pieces—were formed up on the Dyke and beach, connecting the sand-hills of Petten with those of Camperduyn. The infantry stood on the left in column of companies, the artillery in the centre, and the cavalry on the right in column of troops. From this position Sir Ralph Abercromby was to advance along the sea-coast to Egmont-op-Zee, a village situated five miles west of Alkmaar, so as to turn the enemy's left, and then attack the rear of the French posted at Bergen.

The second or centre column was formed entirely of Russians—ten battalions of infantry (averaging 800 bayonets), three troops (about 200 horses) of *hussars* and *Cossack* lancers, and artillery—under Major-General Essen. Of this column, the greater proportion was to move down the Slaper Dyke through the villages of Greet and Schorel, and then by the road skirting the foot of the heights of Camperduyn towards Bergen; the

---

3. Horse artillery were first introduced into the British army in 1793, when four troops were formed by the Duke of Richmond, then Master-General of the Ordnance; two other troops were added in 1794.

remainder, under Major-General Sedmoratzky, were to move off from the Zuype Sluys, in order to cover the left flank of the troops under Essen in their march beneath the sand-hills, and were afterwards to co-operate with the British troops destined for the attack of Schoreldam, and subsequently, if possible, assist in that of Bergen itself.

The third or left column, under Lieutenant-General Dundas, consisted of about 6,000 British troops, including the 2nd, 3rd, and 7th brigades under Major-Generals Burrard, Coote, and the Earl of Chatham, with foot artillery under Lieutenant-Colonel Smith, and two troops of the 11th Light Dragoons under Captain Sleigh. Of these, the 3rd brigade, under Major-General Coote, was to start from Petten with the advance of Abercromby's column, and accompany it to the village of Campe; there it was to turn to the left, so as to take the Slaper Dyke in reverse and dear the road to Groet and the heights above it, by which Major-General Essen was to march.

On the arrival of the Russian column, Major-General Coote was to cover their right in their progress towards Bergen, by detaching a sufficient force into the sand-hills, which here widen out to a breadth of between three and four miles, and then narrow again on the side of Egmont-op-Zee. The 7th brigade, under Lord Chatham, was to move for some distance in rear of the Russian detachment under Major-General Sedmoratzky from Zuype Sluys, and afterwards turn to the right, so as to get into the rear of their main body, under Major-General Essen, and be at hand to assist the 3rd brigade in covering the right of the column. Both the 3rd and 7th brigades were ultimately to assist the Russians in the attack of Bergen, and were also to take ground as much as possible to the right, in order to keep up a communication with the column under Sir Ralph Abercromby, and be at hand for its support, if necessary.

The two battalions of foot-guards forming the 2nd brigade, under Major-General Burrard, were especially destined for the attack on the village of Schoreldam, against which they were to move from Tutenhoorn and Krabbendam, down the left bank

Departure of the Anglo–Russian troops from Den Helder

of the Alkmaar canal. In this service, besides being supported by the Russian corps under Major-General Sedmoratzky, they were to be assisted by Sir Home Popham's flotilla of gun-boats, now increased to seven in number, acting on the Alkmaar canal.

In addition to the three columns intended to act around and against Bergen, a fourth column, consisting of the 5th, 8th, and 9th brigades, under Major-Generals Don, Prince William of Gloucester, and Manners; two battalions of Russian infantry, and two squadrons of the 18th Light Dragoons—in all, 7,000 infantry and 250 cavalry—was placed under the orders of Lieutenant-General Sir James Pulteney. To this officer was assigned the important task of covering the whole of the exposed flank of the army towards the Zuyder Zee, by holding in check the Dutch corps under General Daendels, and preventing him from detaching any troops towards Bergen. He was also to take advantage of any favourable opportunity that might present itself, either to turn the right flank of the enemy's position, or to support with effect the two centre columns. By these dispositions of his army, the Duke of York hoped to be able to force back the French on Haarlem, without giving them time to establish themselves in any intermediate position.

On the right, the column under Lieutenant-General Sir Ralph Abercromby was the first to move. At half-past six o'clock it advanced from Petten, when the reserve, under Colonel Macdonald, pushed along the Sea Dyke, while the main body was conducted by Sir Ralph Abercromby along the beach—the tide having ebbed sufficiently to allow of their passing. Directly after, the reserve gallantly attacked, and carried a redoubt erected by the French in front of Campe, and then followed up their success by forcing the enemy to retire in confusion, both from the village and the sand-hills behind it.

Colonel Macdonald then entered the sand-hills and marched towards their centre, inclining to the left, while the 6th brigade, under Major-General Hutchinson, moved along a ridge of these eminences parallel to the road from Campe to Schoreldam, and the 4th brigade, under Major-General Moore, advanced along their skirts—its right flank keeping close to the edge of the dyke which here borders the sea coast. The main column, under Abercromby himself, consisting of the cavalry, artillery, and 1st brigade of guards, likewise moved forward along the beach below as soon as the advanced brigades had effected an entrance into the sand-hills.

Meanwhile, the 3rd brigade, under Major-General Coote, after following the reserve as far as Campe, had turned off sharp to its left and advanced as far as the extremity of the Slaper Dyke and the village of Groet, so as to leave the road open for the advance of the remainder of the centre column. These were at once put in motion: the Russians, under Major-General Essen, first advanced and deployed on the plain below the sand-hills, and then proceeded to attack the lines before Schorel. In this they were supported by the 7th British brigade, under Lord Chatham, and a squadron of the 11th Light Dragoons, detached for the purpose by Lieutenant-General Dundas. The squadron of the 11th and one Russian battalion led the attack, supported on the side of the sand-hills by the 55th regiment. Fording a deep inundation, the dragoons turned the flank of a breastwork, while the infantry stormed it in front, captured two pieces of artillery, and forced the enemy to retire.

At the same time, a large body of the enemy posted on the heights above Schorel, to the right and front of the Russian column under Major-General Essen, were attacked by Lieutenant-General Dundas, who brought up Coote's brigade from Groet into the sand-hills. After a sharp conflict, the French troops gave way, and retired hastily across the downs, the whole 3rd brigade following in pursuit in advance of the Russian column to the left. Thus assured of the safety of his exposed flank, Major-General Essen moved down the road beneath the sand-hills, and soon became warmly engaged with a large body of French and Dutch troops under General Simon, who had retired from Schorel by degrees as the Russians approached.

They were now formed in line between that village and Schoreldam, and, as the latter came on, received them with a heavy fire, both from their field-pieces and some heavier guns placed on the Koe Dyke. Major-General Essen was soon reinforced, however, by the corps under Major-General Sedmoratzky, which had marched from the Zuype Sluys directly it appeared that the enemy had abandoned Groet, and so left the road open to them. After crossing the plain between the sand-hills and the Alkmaar canal, the Russian infantry under Sedmoratzky formed upon the left of their friends, while, still further to the left, a forward movement was simultaneously effected by Major-General Burrard's brigade.

The 7th brigade, under Major-General the Earl of Chatham, was placed in reserve on the plain, close in rear of Major-General Sedmoratzky's brigade. After some delay, the attack was commenced at about eleven o'clock by the Guards on the left and the Russian column on the right, supported by the fire of the British gun-boats on the Alkmaar canal. After a stout resistance, the enemy were compelled to give way; the Dutch troops of General Dumonceau's division who had defended Schoreldam, retiring on the Koe Dyke, while the French on their left fell back to Bergen and the heights above that village. The whole of the Russian troops then drew up between Schorel and Schoreldam, while Major-General Burrard advanced with the Guards and took possession of Schoreldam.

While these events were passing in the plain, the four regiments composing the 3rd brigade, under Major-General Coote, had pushed on so rapidly in pursuit as to become considerably separated; for while the 2nd Queen's, on the left, were on the heights close above Schorel, the 27th, 29th, and 85th regiments had penetrated a long way into the sand-hills, the latter especially being fax advanced to the right. On their side, the enemy, after several vain attempts to make a stand as they retired towards Bergen, were now considerably reinforced from that place, when they commenced a fierce attack upon the 85th regiment, with the view of turning the flank of the brigade.

As Colonel Macdonald's corps had also inclined considerably to the right, in order to communicate with the main body of Abercromby's column, and was itself warmly engaged with a considerable body of French troops among the sand-hills, no assistance could be obtained from that quarter; and it at first seemed probable that the 85th would be overpowered. Fortunately, the critical position of this regiment—and, indeed, of the whole 3rd brigade—was perceived by the Duke of York, and Lieutenant-General Dundas was at once directed to move the three battalions of the 4th King's Own Regiment, in Lord Chatham's brigade, from the plain into the sand-hills, to reinforce the right of Major-General Coote's brigade, while the 31st regiment were to move close under the hills, in support of its left.

This service was most gallantly performed. On arriving in rear of the 85th regiment, the three battalions of the 4th formed into a line, extending considerably beyond the 85th to the right. They were then led rapidly forward through the scrubby wood and coppice with which the sand-hills are here covered for about three quarters of a mile, so as to gain their summit and turn the enemy's left flank, while the 85th advanced against them in front. Thus attacked on two sides, the enemy abandoned the western ridge of the sand-hills and hastily sought shelter in the thickets on the summit of the heights above Bergen. Thither Lord Chatham at once followed, and then halted, with the three battalions of the 4th regiment; the 85th moving round to the foot of the heights and occupying a defile on the road leading through them into the village. The remaining regiments of the 3rd brigade—the 2nd, 27th, and 29th—now came up and formed on the left of the 4th, and, according to the original plan, a general attack on Bergen should then have taken place, the two British brigades taking the post in reverse, while the Russians moved against it in front.

Major-General Essen, however, declared that he must wait the arrival of Abercromby's column before moving on, and remained inactive between Schorel and Schoreldam; and, for his part, Lieutenant-General Dundas did not consider himself justified in undertaking the attack of the French troops in and around Bergen with a force of seven battalions only. By the hesitation of these officers to advance, General Brune was allowed time to complete his preparations for further resistance along the whole of his left wing. General Gouvion, with all the artillery and two battalions of infantry, was ordered to throw himself into the redoubts to the right of Bergen, and five more battalions, under Generals Simon and Barbou, were directed to support him, while the Adjutant-General, Azèmard, occupied the crest of the sand-hills and the head of the road leading from Bergen to Egmont-op-Zee with three battalions. Four battalions, under Generals Boudet, Fuzier, and Aubrée, lined a long range of sand-hills extending from Bergen right across the plain to the sea, and two more, which had been held in reserve at Alkmaar, were moved towards Egmont-op-Zee.

After taking up the position assigned to them outside Bergen, the French troops under General Gouvion commenced a heavy fire of musketry and artillery, upon the British troops posted on the heights above. The latter had been unable to bring up their field-pieces through the sand-hills, and therefore were not able to return the compliment, so that General Gouvion was encouraged to make an attempt to dislodge them, and so regain possession of the heights. For this purpose, he sent out two strong columns of infantry from the village, one of which moved down the avenue to the left of the place, and gallantly endeavoured to force the pass held by the 85th regiment.

They were, however, driven back with loss; and, in spite of repeated attacks, the 85th succeeded in maintaining their position there during the rest of the day. The other French column, in like manner, passed through the woods, and, at about half-past three o'clock, attacked the 27th regiment, posted at the end of another avenue leading into Bergen. Three companies of the 27th at once made a spirited charge, and drove them back into the woods, with loss. For this service the regiment was thanked in the field by Lord Chatham, who enthusiastically exclaimed, "Twenty-seventh, you have done more than my whole brigade!"

Three battalions of Major-General Coote's brigade were then brought up to the right of Lord Chatham's, to support it and prolong the line from the woods round Bergen, and across the ridges of sand-hills, so as to open a communication with the reserve under Colonel Macdonald. The latter had continued to advance rapidly, bearing down all opposition, until they encountered and soon became warmly engaged with the French brigade under General Azèmard. For some time the reserve were unable to make any impression on the formidable position held by the enemy; perceiving this, Lieutenant-General Dundas sent down the 29th regiment from the left to Colonel Macdonald's assistance; and as soon as that regiment had formed upon the flank of the reserve, it dashed forward to storm the enemy's position.

The other regiments followed from the right, and the whole line crossed the plain without once slackening their speed, although exposed to a terrible discharge of shot, shell, and musketry, and then charged up the steep ascent with such impetuosity as to carry the position and force the enemy to give way on all sides. This terminated the action as far as Lieutenant-General Dundas's column was concerned, although heavy firing was kept up until eleven o'clock at night, between some of the French troops posted in a projection of the wood, and the flank companies of the 3rd brigade. The Russians also, during the whole afternoon, confined themselves to keeping up a heavy cannonade from their artillery, supported by the British gun-boats on the Alkmaar canal, which was returned with spirit by the Dutch troops of General Dumonceau's division, who had fallen back to a strong position on the Koe Dyke, between Schoreldam and Bergen.

While the battle raged during the afternoon in the neighbourhood of Bergen, the main body of the first column, under Lieutenant-General Sir Ralph Abercromby, had continued its advance along the beach for between six and seven miles, without meeting with any interruption from the enemy. Since quitting the extremity of the Sea Dyke, it had been compelled to reduce its front, the beach being very narrow from the tide having not yet subsided; and as it was, the right flank of the cavalry was continually in the water. By this time, also, the infantry had become much distressed and fatigued by the heavy nature of the soil, into which they sank up to their ankles at every step. At this juncture, a body of French riflemen lined the sand-hills to the left, and commenced a scattering fire on the British column.

Very soon these were considerably reinforced, and commenced to gall the troops from every eminence and outlet of the surrounding sand-hills. This annoyance was kept up until the column had advanced four miles further, by which time the 4th brigade, and especially the 25th regiment—which formed the advance, under Lieutenant-Colonel Wright—had suffered heavily, many of the officers being picked off by the enemy's sharpshooters. Regiment after regiment had been detached from the main column into the hills to make head against the French, who were rapidly increasing in numbers, until only the 3rd battalion 1st Guards and the 92nd Highlanders remained with the cavalry and artillery on the beach.

The French then brought forward two field-pieces from Egmont-op-Zee, which they planted on a considerable eminence, so as to command the hills in advance and overlook the beach, and then opened fire both upon the column of infantry and upon the cavalry, who had already suffered severely from the fire of their riflemen in the sand-hills. At this critical moment, the two columns of Generals Boudet and Fuzier appeared from the direction of Bergen, and took up a position on some heights in front of Egmont-op-Zee, which form a sort of amphitheatre towards the coast, while several squadrons of French cavalry were drawn up on the beach to their left. Favoured by the strength of their position, this corps—about 6,000 strong—appeared determined to resist the further advance of the British column.

On the part of the British, the attack was commenced by the 4th brigade, under Major-General Moore, which endeavoured to carry the sand-hills at the point of the bayonet, but the French infantry stood firm, and repulsed their assailants. The engagement was then continued for several hours with the greatest obstinacy on both sides. The British infantry on the sand-hills were exhausted by fatigue and want of water, and were beaten back in every attempt to storm the enemy's position; nevertheless, they continued to fight with unabated fury, and preserved their good order and discipline, in spite of the incessant fire which so fearfully thinned their ranks. Lieutenant-General Sir Ralph Abercromby had two horses killed under him; Major-General Moore was shot through the thigh, but continued on the field for nearly two hours, until absolutely forced to quit it by a second wound in the face; and the Marquis of Huntly received a rifle ball in the shoulder while leading the 92nd to the charge. That regiment, indeed, lost nearly all its officers and men before the least impression seemed to have been made on the enemy.

At length, late in the afternoon, the British infantry, advancing from their left under a tremendous fire of musketry, succeeded in gaining a footing on the road leading from Egmont-op-Zee to Bergen, so as to cut off the enemy's extreme left from their communication with the rest of their army. On hearing of this, General Brune, who still remained at Bergen to hold in check the main body of the British and Russian forces, at once directed General Daendels to send two battalions of Dutch infantry and 100 *hussars* to Egmont-op-Zee by way of Alkmaar, while three other battalions were brought up to guard the approach to Bergen. He also dispatched General Vandamme to take command at the former place.

On arriving at Egmont-op-Zee, this officer found that the French infantry had been forced to give way, when he resolved to make a bold effort to retrieve the fortune of the day, by turning the right of the British line. At this time, the guns of the latter had been necessarily advanced on that side to check the French artillery, and were only guarded by a squadron of the 15th Light Dragoons; the rest of the cavalry under Lord Paget having retired into a ravine between two of the sand-hills, where they could not be seen from the French position. This caused

Vandamme to suppose that the capture of the guns might be easily effected, and, for that purpose, he put himself at the head of 500 French cavalry, and charged gallantly down a distance of half a mile in the face of the whole of the British infantry. As this body of horsemen came sweeping towards them along the beach, the British horse artillery, under Major Judson, opened on them, but without effect, and directly after the French troopers were among the guns, fighting hand to hand with the artillerymen, and cutting them down.

Two of the guns were, for a few moments, completely in their possession, but then the squadron of the 15th came up, dashed into the thickest of the enemy, and drove them back from the guns. Recovering from the confusion caused by this unexpected check, the French cavalry rallied, and had again advanced to within forty yards of the 15th, who had reformed in front of their guns to prevent their being carried off, when the third troop of the 15th, which had been ordered to advance, came up, charged the French, and drove them back half a mile. The rest of the British cavalry, under Lord Paget, now arrived at a gallop, and followed the enemy towards Egmont-op-Zee, when, as it was now nearly six o'clock in the evening, the action ceased on the side of the beach.

Further to the left, two battalions from the reserve, under Colonel Macdonald, had arrived to the support of the infantry under Abercromby, and became immediately engaged; so that, at about seven o'clock, the enemy were forced to yield up their well-defended position, and draw off towards Beverwyck. As, however, Bergen was known to be still in possession of the enemy, Sir Ralph Abercromby considered that he had advanced far enough, and, therefore, determined to take up a position for the night, instead of pushing on to Egmont-op-Zee. Orders were, therefore, given for this purpose, and the infantry formed a line upon the sand-hills, the cavalry prolonging it across the beach to the right. There the troops lay upon their arms until morning, exposed the whole time to a dropping fire of shells from some French artillery, placed about 1000 yards off.

In addition to this annoyance, both men and horses at first suffered greatly from want of water; for, in the morning, the great heat had caused the men to have such frequent recourse to their water bottles, that they were emptied by the middle of the day, and, on halting for the night, they had to dig wells in the sand to replenish them, and so quench the excessive thirst created by the rations of salt meat, which now only they could find time to eat. In one or two places a little water was thus obtained, but the rush to the spot was so great as to prevent many from partaking of it; and these were thus compelled to lie down in all the agonies of thirst, until a heavy shower of rain came down and afforded the relief desired.

Throughout this eventful day, the left column, under Lieutenant-General Sir James Pulteney, although it had no such opportunities of distinguishing itself as fell to the share of the centre and right, was nevertheless most usefully employed in menacing the principal post of the Dutch troops at Oude-Carspel, from its own position in front of Drixhoorn. By this means, it was rendered impossible for General Daendels to detach any considerable body of Dutch troops to the assistance of the French army on his left, although he was fully aware how much they were there required.

During the night succeeding the action. General Brune, who regarded his position at Bergen as untenable, now that Abercromby had succeeded in forcing his left, and that the heights above the place were for three miles in possession of the British infantry, gave orders for a retreat of the whole Gallo-Batavian army. The greater part of the French army, accordingly, retired from Bergen during the night; but one brigade, under General Gouvion, remained in the woods about the place, and another, under General Bonhomme, with artillery, between it and the Koe Dyke. At eight o'clock next morning, these two brigades, with the cavalry, under General Simon, drew off across the plain in the direction of Alkmaar, while General Daendels simultaneously evacuated Oude-Carspel and his other posts on the Lange Dyke, and fell back with the main body of the Dutch army,

8,000 strong, by way of St. Pancras and beyond Alkmaar to Purmerend. In the afternoon, a brigade, left at Egmont-op-Zee to cover the retreat of the centre, was likewise withdrawn by General Boudet.

The different posts thus abandoned by the enemy were occupied at different times during the day, by the British and Russian troops. On the left, Sir James Pulteney occupied Oude- Carspel and the Lange Dyke soon after daybreak; and Prince William of Gloucester, rapidly advancing to Schemerhorn in pursuit of General Daendels, captured three field-pieces, which the latter had abandoned on the road. Bergen was occupied at noon by the 85th regiment, and in the evening the Russian corps under Major-General Essen moved forward from the position it had occupied during the night, between Schorel and Schoreldam to the village of Egmont-op-te-Hoof. On the left of the Russians Major-General Burrard advanced to the Koe Dyke. Earlier in the day, a small party of the 18th Light Dragoons, under Captain Harcourt, had ventured towards Alkmaar, where they surrounded and forced to surrender a strong picquet belonging to the rear-guard of the French army.

The town itself had been abandoned by the enemy, who were discovered to be in full retreat towards the pass of Beverwyck, their last position in North Holland; and the inhabitants now hastened to hoist the Orange flag, set ringing the bells of the cathedral, and throw open their gates to the detachment of the 18th. The latter then kept possession of the place for several hours, at the expiration of which they were reinforced by a detachment of the foot-guards from Major-General Burrard's brigade. On the right of the British army, it had been the intention of Sir Ralph Abercromby to move forward at daybreak; but the troops were found to be so exhausted from want of food, that it was decided that the advance should not take place until they had been refreshed. In consequence of the bad state of the roads, neither the bread nor the waggons for the wounded arrived before four o'clock in the afternoon; an order was then issued for the regiments to send for their rations; but before it could be obeyed, intelligence arrived of the retreat of the French under General Vandamme from Egmont-op-Zee.

Not a moment was to be lost; the troops were ordered under arms, and at once moved forward, leaving their provisions untasted on the beach. On entering Egmont-op-Zee, the French were found to have retired two hours before, and nothing was seen of them, although the pursuit was continued three miles. As soon, therefore, as the advanced posts had been established, the infantry went into cantonments, in barns and huts, but the cavalry again lay all night on the beach, the men and horses remaining frilly equipped, and suffering much inconvenience from want of fresh water. Some of the horses were actually sixty, and all the others at least fifty, hours without either hay or water. In the centre of the army, the exhausted state of the troops, from having been so many hours under arms, prevented any attempt to harass the enemy in their retreat beyond Alkmaar.

The occupation by the British troops of the entire position recently held by the enemy; the occupation of Alkmaar, the capital of North Holland; and the consequent recovery to the House of Orange of the whole of that province—these were the results of the second battle of Bergen, or, as it is called for the sake of distinction, the Battle of Alkmaar. The victory, however, was hardly won, for not less than 2,200 British and Russians were killed and wounded; of this heavy loss, by far the greater proportion fell to the share of the former, as the Russians were in comparison but slightly engaged. Major Lumsden, 55th regiment, ten officers of inferior rank, and 226 non-commissioned officers and men, were slain; Major-General Moore, Colonels Cameron, of the 79th, and the Marquis of Huntly, of the 92nd Highlanders, five other field officers, 62 captains and subalterns, 1,033 non-commissioned officers and men, wounded; 5 officers and 188 non-commissioned officers and men taken prisoners.

The 92nd Highlanders, who were so especially distinguished in this action, suffered severely, losing 14 officers and 278 men; the 25th regiment also had one-third of the officers present and one-fourth of its men killed, wounded, or taken. In the Russian corps, 4 officers and 166 men killed or taken, and Major-General Emmé, 19 other officers, and 403 men, wounded. On the other hand, the total loss of the Gallo-Batavian army was about 3,000, and they also left behind on the field seven pieces of artillery and a number of tumbrils. The prisoners, 300 in number, were sent off to the Helder, to be embarked for Great Britain. A considerable number of deserters from the Dutch army to the standard of the Prince of Orange, who had come over on hearing of the defeat of their Dutch allies, were also forwarded to the Helder, to be incorporated with the regiments forming there for his service.[4]

The following regiments, which were in Lieutenant-General Sir Ralph Abercromby's column, bear the honorary distinction, "Egmont-op-Zee," on their guidons, colours, and appointments—15th Light Dragoons, 1st Royals, 20th regiment, 25th King's Own Borderers, 49th and 63rd regiments, 79th and 92nd Highlanders.

---

4. For details of loss in the British and Russian armies, nominal lists of officers, &c., see Appendix No. 9; and for the Duke of York's General Order on the occasion of the victory, No. 10.

CHAPTER 4

The Battle of Egmont

After the Battle of Alkmaar, fought on the 2nd of October, and their consequent retreat from their position in front of that town, the Gallo-Batavian army, under General Brune, occupied a line of defence more contracted, and therefore proportionally stronger, than that from which they had been driven. This new line of defence crossed the isthmus which connects the two provinces of North and South Holland, extending from the town of Beverwyck, situated at the head of the Wye or Y, as the inlet of the Zuyder Zee, which renders North Holland almost a peninsula, is called, to the village of Wyck-op-Zee, on the German Ocean. This isthmus, although seven miles in depth from Beverwyck to the city of Haarlem, is only three miles across from the same town to Wyck-op-Zee.

In this narrow and exceedingly defensible position. General Brune possessed complete command of the water communication between the head of the Wye and the lake of Haarlem, which consists of a series of locks and canals of such stupendous construction, that all the waters of the Zuyder Zee might be poured down through them on the southern provinces. By this means, he was enabled to bring up supplies with great facility both from Haarlem and from Amsterdam, the latter city situated only a few miles south-east of the lake, to which the former gives its name. On the arrival of a reinforcement of six battalions from Belgium, the French troops were organized in two divisions, which General Brune entrusted to Generals Gouvion and

Boudet, under the chief direction of General Vandamme.

The first division was placed between Wyck-op-Zee and Heemskurkduyn, with its left well protected by the sand-hills and the sea, and the second on its right, near Wergeist. Of the Dutch army, Dumonceau's division, under General Bonhomme, was placed in front of Beverwyck, extending from the Lang-meer to Acker-Sloot, while their advanced posts, under General Pacthod, were extended through that village, Limmen and Bac-cum, down to the coast. Finally, General Daendels was charged with the defence of the inundated Polders, for which purpose he took post at Monnikendam and Purmerend, with his right towards Knollendam. The reserve, formed of two *demi*-brigades under General Fuzier, remained at Beverwyck, while a great part of the baggage of the army was sent off to Haarlem.

As soon as he had obtained accurate information regard-ing the new position taken up by the Gallo-Batavian army, the British commander-in-chief decided to attack their left in the intrenchments at Beverwyck, since their right was rendered un-assailable by the inundations, and, if possible, force them to re-tire further to the southward, before they should receive farther reinforcements from France. By these means, he hoped to make himself master of Haarlem, and so obtain a suitable *depôt* for his army, and, at the same time, to cut off all communication by land, between the French and their Dutch allies. At present, the Duke of York's own headquarters were at Alkmaar, and a part of the troops were housed in that town, while the remainder were disposed in the villages and farmhouses, along a line extending on either side to the German Ocean and the Zuyder Zee. The advanced posts were so arranged during the 3rd and 4th of Oc-tober as to form a line parallel to those of the Gallo-Batavian army.

On the right, those of Abercromby's division had been pushed forward below Egmont-op-Zee, and those of the Russian corps, under Major-General Essen, in front of Egmont-Brunen and Egmont-op-te-Hoof. In the centre, the village of Heyloo, lying between Alkmaar and Limmen, was occupied by a detachment from the division under Lieutenant-General Dundas, while, on the left, the 8th brigade, under Prince William of Gloucester, had been detached by Lieutenant-General Sir James Pulteney to reoccupy the town of Hoorn. The rest of Pulteney's column remained concentrated between Schemerhorn and Alkmaar, behind a number of canals, which unite at Saardam, 11 miles due-west of the latter town, and there have one common outlet into the Zuyder Zee.

In this position, the situation of the British and Russian forces was still far from satisfactory, for no provisions could be obtained in the country, and it was, therefore, necessary to bring up supplies of every description from the shipping, an operation rendered extremely difficult by the want of proper transport, the distance from the Helder, and the bad state of the roads, which were rendered all but impassable by the recent heavy rains, and the consequent overflowing of the numerous canals. Moreover, the insalubrity of the climate was already beginning to tell upon the troops, whose whole available force had been reduced by garrisons furnished for Medemblick and Enkhuysen, and other detachments, by casualties in the field, and by the numerous sick, to about 27,000 effectives, while there seemed no probability of any assistance to the cause of their rightful sovereign being afforded by the Dutch people.

Preparatory, therefore, to the contemplated attack upon the enemy's position, a general movement of the advanced posts of the centre and right of the army was ordered, and put into execution on the morning of the 6th of October. On the left, Major-General Coote, with the 3rd brigade, advanced from Bergen by Alkmaar, and through the village of Heyloo upon Limmen, which was speedily carried, while two French battalions, which held the village of Acker-Sloot, were dislodged, with the loss of 200 prisoners, and forced to retire on General Bonhomme's division at Wergest, by four companies of the 3rd and one of the Coldstream Guards, under Colonel Clephane, detached from Major-General Burrard's brigade. The Russians, under Major-General Essen, were equally successful at Baccum, the defenders of that village, which, with Limmen and Acker-Sloot, formed a chain of posts extending along the front of the enemy's lines at Beverwyck, falling back towards Castricum, while the ground between Baccum and the sea was occupied by the reserve under Colonel Macdonald, whose picquets of half battalions had lain all night on the sand-hills, in advance of the enemy's left at Wyck-op-Zee.

Thus far, and no farther, it was intended that these corps should proceed, there being no intention on the part of the British commander-in-chief to follow up this partial success, by attacking the enemy's entrenchments. Unfortunately, Major- General Essen, after occupying Baccum with the Russian troops, decided to push on to the attack of Castricum, the possession of which village he considered essential to the safety of his position. In this attempt, he was at first vigorously opposed by three French battalions under General Pacthod; but, on the appearance of Abercromby's column moving along the coast on their flank, the latter gave way, and fell back from Castricum into the sand-hills beyond. Elated at their success, the Russians followed, and attacked the French brigade in their new position; but General Pacthod resisted gallantly, and so gave time to General Brune to order up a division, under General Boudet, to his support, while General Gouvion was directed to manoeuvre in the sand-hills, so as to engage the attention of the British on that side.

By the time that the leading battalion of Boudet's division came up, the Russians had almost succeeded in forcing General Pacthod to retreat once more; but now the sides became more even, and the engagement raged for three hours without any decided advantage to either. At last, General Brune, after detaching three battalions to hold Abercromby's corps in check, led forward the rest of his infantry in close columns of battalions, and, charging the Russians with the bayonet, drove them back in disorder from the sand-hills to Castricum. There, Major-General Essen was joined by Sir Ralph Abercromby, at the head of the British reserve, from the sand-hills on his right; and, thus supported, he promptly rallied about 4,000 men, and disposed his artillery so as to sweep the approaches to the village. Scarcely were these arrangements completed, when the brigade under General Pacthod, supported by General Boudet's division, attacked in its turn.

After a long and obstinate struggle, the French succeeded in capturing the field-pieces placed at the entrances to the place, and their heavy columns of infantry forced their way into its streets. The Russians then gave way, and retired along the roads to Baccum and Limmen, Pacthod's infantry following towards the latter village, while Barbou's cavalry swept over the sand-hills towards Baccum. A total rout would probably have ensued, had it not been for some squadrons of the 7th and 11th Light Dragoons, which charged out from a gorge of the sand-hills, with Lord Paget at their head, and put to flight a dragoon regiment, which formed the advance of the French cavalry. The disorder thus occasioned, communicated itself to the rest of the column, and the whole of Barbou's brigade fled precipitately to the heights of Castricum, involving in their flight the infantry under General Pacthod, who had been stayed in their onward progress by the Russians breaking down the bridge of Schilpwater, and placing what guns they retained to command it.

Time was thus allowed to Major-General Essen to reform his troops, and on being supported by two English battalions, sent up by Lieutenant-General Dundas, he re-established the bridge, passed over again, and attacked Castricum on one side, while the British reserve assailed it from another. The French and Dutch troops there, being overcome with fatigue and short of ammunition, soon gave way, pursued by the Russian infantry, while two squadrons of the 11th Light Dragoons, under Captain Sleigh, advanced to turn the enemy's left. At this juncture, when a total defeat of his army seemed imminent. General Brune himself brought up some squadrons of Dutch hussars, charged the British cavalry and forced them back upon the infantry, so that Essen, unable to maintain the ground he had gained, was forced to fell back towards Baccum with considerable loss.

While the combat was continued with so great fury in the centre, the corps under Sir Ralph Abercromby, on the right, was engaged with the French left wing, under General Gouvion. After a sharp conflict between the advanced posts, in which the British troops sustained some loss from the fire of the enemy's artillery, Major-General Hutchinson led the Earl of Cavan's brigade into the sand-hills, to cut off one French brigade, under General Simon, from another, under General Aubrée. Perceiving Hutchinson's object. General Gouvion anticipated him by entering the sand-hills with such troops as he had hitherto kept in reserve; the whole French left wing then advancing, the British troops were forced back in succession from all the posts they had occupied, until they reached the heights south of the villages of Egmont. Here both British and Russians made a determined stand, and frustrated every attempt of General Brune to drive them farther.

The shades of evening closing over the field produced no cessation of hostilities; for then Abercromby, reinforced from the left by the British reserve, which had been acting in co-operation with the Russians, made another attempt to regain his lost ground; but Gouvion, who had taken up a position on the heights of Baccum, resisted all his efforts, and maintained himself there until ten o'clock, when General Brune issued orders for a general retreat, and the whole of his troops consequently fell back to their former position in front of Beverwyck, leaving the British and Russians masters of the field of battle. On the left of the latter, Major-General Coote, with the 3rd brigade and some field-pieces and howitzers, had succeeded in maintaining himself the whole day in the village of Limmen, in spite of repeated efforts made by the enemy to dislodge him; but the immense inundations which covered the front of the main body of the Dutch troops, under General Daendels, prevented Lieutenant-General Sir James Pulteney from effecting anything against them.

In the course of the day, Major-General Don was sent by Sir James Pulteney to the Dutch general, with some message relative to an exchange of prisoners, under protection of a flag of truce. As Major-General Don endeavoured to circulate a proclamation which had a tendency to excite the Dutch soldiers against their French allies, Daendels sent him as a prisoner to General Brune, who caused him to be conveyed to the citadel of Liege. There he remained in close confinement, until exchanged in the month of June, 1800.

In this indecisive engagement, which has been generally known as the Battle of Egmont, the loss of both the British and Russian troops was very severe. Of the former, over 1,400 (including 70 officers) were killed, wounded, or made prisoners; this loss fell chiefly on the three battalions of the 4th regiment, the two battalions of the 20th, and the 31st and 63rd regiments. Lieutenant-Colonels Dickson, 2nd battalion 4th, and Bainbridge, 1st battalion 20th, were both slain; Major-General Hutchinson received a musket-shot in the leg, and Lieutenant-Colonel Hodgson, 1st battalion 4th, Colonel Maitland, of the 1st Foot Guards, and Major Campbell, 1st battalion 20th, were also wounded, the two latter so badly, that they died a few days after; while Lieutenant-Colonels Lake, of the 1st Guards, and Cholmondeley, 2nd battalion 4th, were made prisoners, a great part of his own and the 3rd battalion being taken along with the latter.

The loss of the Russians amounted to eight officers and 374 non-commissioned officers and men killed or missing, and 26 officers and 709 non-commissioned officers and men wounded.[5] The blame of the reverse at Castricum was justly attributed to them, as by their rash advance to that place, they brought on a general action, when the intention of the British commander-in-chief was merely to approach nearer to the enemy's position, in order to attack it next day to greater advantage.

The British and Russian troops lay on their arms during the night succeeding the battle, and next morning found themselves in a most dangerous position. The different corps were dispersed

---

5. *Vide* Appendix No. 11, for lists of killed, wounded, and missing, names of officers, &c.

over a wide expanse of country, without order or support. The right wing, under Sir Ralph Abercromby, lay in Egmont-op-Zee; the Russians, under Essen, were in Egmont-op-te-Hoof, and the left wing at Heyloo and the villages south of Alkmaar. Since the preceding evening, the weather had set in with renewed inclemency, and the rain came down in torrents. The whole army lay exposed on the open sand-hills, their arms and ammunition spoiled, and their clothes saturated with rain-water.

During the day, the soldiers were busily employed in preparing some kind of shelter on the sand-hills against the night—such as constructing sheds of rushes, and digging trenches in the sand. On the other hand, the enemy, confident in the strength of their position, and elated at the indisputable success they had obtained the day before, and at the arrival of two French *demi*-brigades, amounting to 6,000 infantry, who amply compensated for their loss of 2,000 killed and wounded, now advanced a strong body of troops to the town of Purmerend, not far from the British left. At Purmerend this corps took up an almost impregnable position, covered by an inundation, while all the avenues of approach were held by their detachments; so that, were the allied army to advance, it would be able to act with effect either on their left flank or on their rear.

Moreover, even were the Duke of York to succeed in carrying the position of Beverwyck, there were several points, all strongly fortified and capable of stout resistance, on the isthmus in rear of it, which it would be necessary for him to carry before Haarlem could be attacked; while General Brune was expecting further strong reinforcements from the Directory, now relieved from the apprehensions they had been under for their own territory, by the Austrian army, under the Archduke Charles, taking up a defensive position on the Rhine.

Under these circumstances, the Duke of York summoned a council of war, composed of the lieutenant-generals of his army, whose unanimous opinion was that it would be impossible for the army longer to maintain itself in its present advanced position, and that it should be withdrawn to its original position on the Zuype—now distant nearly 30 miles—there to await orders from England. On this opinion the commander-in-chief decided to act, and at seven the same evening orders were unexpectedly issued for the regiments to get under arms, and form up by brigades. This was only effected with much delay and terrible confusion and difficulty, occasioned by the incessant rain and the darkness of the evening. Fires were lighted on the heights where the advanced picquets had been posted, in order to deceive the French outposts as to what was going on; and by ten o'clock the whole army was in full retreat, leaving at Egmont-op-Zee about 40 wounded, who were not in a condition to be removed.[6]

The right wing took the route along the beach to Petten, while the rest of the army fell back by way of Alkmaar. The extreme peril of their situation—since, were the enemy to discover their retrograde movement, it was well known that the most disastrous consequences would ensue—had at first a salutary effect upon both British and Russian battalions, and caused them to move with some degree of order, until they drew near the line of the Zuype. Then, however, a scene of disorder ensued, each regiment making the best of its way to its allotted station by the nearest road, and in this way many soldiers lost their corps, and could not find them again during the rest of the march. By the evening of the 8th, the main body of the army had regained their old position on the great dyke of the Zuype, when the Duke of York's headquarters were again established at Schagenbrug,[7] and the advanced posts of the army on the right, centre, and left, fixed at Petten, Drixhoorn, and Winckel.

During the following day a number of stragglers continued to drop in, but between 500 and 600 others had fallen into the hands of some squadrons of *chasseurs-à-cheval*, whom General Brune had sent in pursuit, as soon as the Duke of York's retreat was, rather tardily, discovered. Some baggage-waggons, and about 300 British soldiers' wives, who had accompanied the

6. *Vide* Appendix No. 12.
7. *Vide* Appendix No. 13.

army, were also taken by the French cavalry; the latter were sent to Amsterdam, but released three days after, after being kindly treated and presented with new clothes by the citizens.

No sooner did the Gallo-Batavian commander-in-chief discover that the British and Russian forces had actually withdrawn the whole distance to the Zuype, than he gave directions for a simultaneous forward movement of his whole army. On the 8th of October, accordingly, its left and centre divisions entered Alkmaar, and again took up the positions they had occupied before the action of the 2nd, and in the evening their light troops appeared in front of Petten and Krabbendam. Next day General Brune re-established his headquarters at Alkmaar, and occupied Warmanhuysen and Drixhoorn with detachments, while his cavalry scoured the country to within cannon-shot of the British advanced posts. On his right, the Dutch troops, under General Daendels, entered Hoorn, from which the 8th brigade, under Prince William of Gloucester, forming the rear-guard of the British left wing, had retreated to the village of Winckel, and there taken post behind the canal called the Verlaat. Next day General Daendels advanced from Hoorn, and, on being joined by General Dumonceau's brigade, he resolved to commence offensive operations by attacking Prince William at Winckel.

Accordingly, the whole Dutch force, amounting to about 6,000 men, with 15 pieces of artillery, was put in motion at about 11 o'clock, in order to force the passage of the Verlaat, to defend which Prince William had only about 1,050 effective bayonets, with two six-pounders and one howitzer. Nevertheless, the assailants met with a gallant resistance. On their left, General Bonhomme, who advanced at the head of four battalions, supported by General Dumonceau, was repulsed in an attempt to carry a bridge across the canal, with the loss of 100 men killed and wounded and 13 made prisoners, by six companies of the 2nd battalion 35th regiment, under Lieutenant-Colonel Massey, directed by Prince William himself, who were drawn up in some fields to the right of the bridge, and were supported at about one o'clock, when the action was nearly over, by a single field-piece detached from Winckel.[8]

Meanwhile, Daendels himself, with not less than 5,000 men, had advanced against the British left, consisting of the 1st and 2nd battalions 5th regiment, together scarcely 600 strong, which were posted in front of the village, under cover of a small redoubt erected upon the dyke of the Verlaat. To cover the exposed flank of the brigade, this dyke had been cut across to a depth of nine feet. Owing to their great numerical superiority, the Dutch troops shortly succeeded in forcing a passage across the canal, but then Lieutenant-Colonel Bligh, in command of the 1st battalion 5th, who had promptly perceived that were the enemy allowed to advance further the retreat of the brigade would be cut off, planted the colours, as a rallying point for his regiment, on the top of the dyke, and maintained his ground there until he had secured and covered the retreat of the remainder of the British force.

The 2nd battalions 5th and 35th had also maintained their positions, until ordered to retreat by Prince William, in consequence of orders received from the commander-in-chief, when the whole brigade were brought off, with their guns, ammunition, and baggage, with the loss of only 3 killed and 12 wounded. No attempt was made to harass it in its retreat, and by nightfall it arrived at Oude Sluys.[9]

Once in possession of Winckel, the approach to Schagenbrug lay open to the enemy; so that, to ensure his possession of the latter place, the Duke of York was forced to inundate a small tract of country to the eastward. On their side, the Gallo-Batavian army occupied, on the 12th and 13th October, all the ground immediately in front of the British lines on the Zuype. Their left, composed of French troops, lay before Petten; and their

8. *Military Calendar*, vol. i.
9. On this occasion Prince William issued the following Brigade Order:—
Oude Sluys, 12th October, 1799.
"Prince William desires Col. Bligh and the 1st battalion of the 5th regiment will accept his thanks for the gallant manner in which they attacked the enemy when he was passing the canal opposite Winckel, and Lieutenant-Colonels Talbot and Lindsay, of the 2nd battalion of the 5th, for their exertions on the 10th instant."—Cannon's Historical Record of the 5th Northumberland Fusiliers.

centre, also French, at Warmanhuysen and Drixhoorn, while on the right the Dutch division under General Dumonceau re-established a line of communication with the column under General Daendels, by taking possession of the village of Hee-renscapel. Daendels himself, having pushed on as far as Luth-winckel, took post at the sluice of Zeedyke.

These dispositions seeming to indicate an attempt on their part to assail his position, the Duke of York lost no time in strengthening it as much as possible, and in sending to the Texel Island or to England the sick and wounded of his army. To Eng-land were also removed the Dutch levies forming at the Helder for the Prince of Orange. On the other hand, detachments of troops continued to drop in—three troops of the 15th light dra-goons, under Lieutenant-Colonel Anson, having arrived at the Helder from Ramsgate on the 10th October. A fourth squadron of the 15th were under orders to follow, but the news of the retreat to the lines of Zuype caused their departure to be coun-termanded; not, however, until they had actually gone on board the transports in Ramsgate harbour.

While the events above narrated were passing on shore, the efforts of the British flotilla in the Zuyder Zee, and on other parts of the Dutch coast, were continued with unabated vigour and uniform success, a number of gunboats and several light ships of war being taken from the enemy. The town of Lemmer, in West Friesland, was also gallantly defended by a body of sea-men and marines, about 157 of all ranks, which had been landed from the flotilla to act as a garrison under the orders of Captain Boorder, of the *Espiègle*, 16 gun sloop. To effect the reduction of Lemmertown, a column of 700 men, with two guns, had been detached from the Gallo-Batavian army, and arrived before the place on the 10th October.

At five o'clock on the following morning, a mixed party of French and Dutch volunteers advanced to storm the north bat-tery; but in this endeavour they were surrounded by the Brit-ish seamen, armed with pikes, two of their number killed, and the rest—consisting of one officer, one sergeant, and 27 rank and file— compelled to surrender. No sooner had the prisoners been secured than the rest of the French and Batavian troops assailed the place at all points, and for four hours and a half the contest was sustained most obstinately on both sides.

At the end of that time, the enemy, having lost five men killed and nine wounded, gave way and retired precipitately, breaking down a bridge on their road to prevent pursuit. Had they not taken this precaution, their two field-pieces and colours would probably have fallen into the possession of the British marines, who followed them as far as the bridge; and, as it was, no less than 18 of the fugitives were killed and 20 wounded there by the repeated volleys of the latter. Their total loss thus amounted to 25 killed and 29 wounded, while in the little garrison not a man was wounded.

By the middle of October, the season in North Holland began to assume the aspect of an early and rigorous winter, and it became evident that the British commander-in-chief, since the resumption of active hostilities was thus rendered utterly out of the question, must now decide whether he would continue to act on the defensive in his present position, or endeavour to evacuate it by some means or other. The former alternative was soon set aside, since it was pronounced impossible that the combined British and Russian forces, still about 30,000 strong, could be subsisted until spring upon such supplies as were to be obtained within the limits of the confined and impoverished district they at present occupied—harassed, moreover, as they would be, in front by an active and enterprising enemy, provided with every requisite for carrying on a winter campaign.

It was, therefore, ultimately decided that the whole of the British and Russian troops should be withdrawn from North Holland to England, as soon as possible. To carry out this resolution it seemed necessary to adopt one of two courses—either to flood the country in front of the line of the Zuype and to fortify the heights above the Helder so as to cover the embarkation, or to enter into negotiations with the enemy in order to prevail on them not to hinder it. With regard to the former, the possession of the sluices at Colhorn, Oude Sluys, and Petten, gave the British general the complete command of the waters both of the German Ocean and of the Zuyder Zee, so that it would be easy for him to interpose a wide sheet of water between his own and the Gallo-Batavian army, and then convey the former without molestation on board the transports at the Helder.

To avail himself of this power, however, would have been to lay waste the country and ruin the unfortunate inhabitants, whose deliverance from the power of France had been one of the main objects of the expedition; and it was remembered that the enemy had never made any attempt to inundate the district north of Alkmaar, either for the protection of that town or to cover their own retreat. At the same time, it was clear that, should an inundation not be carried out, it would be very dangerous to trust solely to works thrown up on the heights of Huysduinen or round the Helder; as, should the enemy once succeed in forcing those works, the troops then embarking would be at their mercy.

Acting on these considerations, therefore, the Duke of York gave up all idea of adopting such a desperate alternative as that of inundating the country, and resolved instead to open negotiations, with a view to bringing about a suspension of hostilities between the two armies. On the 14th of October, therefore, he sent a message, under cover of a flag of truce, to General Brune at Alkmaar, expressing his desire to retreat; to this message the latter returned a favourable answer; and, in consequence, Major-General Knox was next morning despatched as a commissioner to the French headquarters, with instructions to arrange the terms of a capitulation with their adjutant-general, Rostolan. Elated at having, as they considered, forced the British commander-in-chief to sue for terms, the demands of the enemy were at first most unreasonable; for General Brune proposed and insisted that the entire Batavian fleet taken at the Texel should be restored, and that 15,000 of the French and Dutch soldiers and seamen, then prisoners in England, should be given up without exchange.

The first demand was peremptorily rejected by the Duke of York, even to the extent of authorising Major-General Knox to break off the negotiation should it be further insisted on; but, as it was considered expedient to give up a certain number of prisoners of war in order to obtain an uninterrupted embarkation for his own troops, it was ultimately settled that 8,000 should be restored without conditions to their respective countries. All prisoners taken by both sides during the present campaign were also to be given up, those on parole as well as others; and the liberation of the Dutch admiral, De Winter, who had been taken at Camperdown, was agreed to by a special article. It was further arranged that the British and Russian troops should embark as soon as possible, and that the whole should quit the territories, coasts, and lands of the Batavian Republic by the last day of November; while the ordnance and military stores which the army under the Duke of York had captured at the Helder and other places, now held by them, were to be left in their present state for the Dutch Government.

On the 18th of October the agreement was finally concluded, at Alkmaar, and was immediately followed by a suspension of hostilities—Major-General Knox being left as a hostage with the enemy, until all the stipulations of the convention should have been fulfilled. On the 22nd, the first of the troops, being detachments of cavalry, began to embark at the Nieuwe Diep, and they were speedily followed by others, who marched successively down to the Helder as the transports were prepared for their reception: at the same time the British flotilla withdrew from its station near the principal towns of the Zuyder Zee.

At Enchuysen, Vice-Admiral Mitchell attempted to destroy the timber and dockyards, with some armed vessels and ships belonging to the Dutch East India Company, which could not be brought off. This measure he justified in a suitable address to the inhabitants, threatening also to destroy the town, should the magistrates installed there in the name of the Prince of Orange be molested. Unfortunately, a detachment of Batavian troops arrived in time to save part of the ships, after which they restored the republican municipality and sent the provisional regency to prison.

On the 1st of November, the commander-in-chief, after giving over the command of the remaining troops to Lieutenant-General Sir James Pulteney, and sending his chargers as a present to General Brune, embarked in the *Juno* frigate, which sailed immediately for Yarmouth, and landed him there after a stormy passage of two days; and, by the 20th of November, the whole of the British and Russian forces, together with nearly 4,000 Dutch loyalists and deserters, had departed from the Texel. The Russians were sent to Jersey and Guernsey; one of their detachments, which was on board *L'Espion* frigate, armed *en flûte*, was wrecked on the Goodwin Sands on the 15th of November, but the troops and crew were saved by the Deal and Ramsgate boats.

The reports of their behaviour during the recent campaign proved so unsatisfactory to the Emperor Paul, that he thought proper to signify his displeasure to the whole of the corps, and to deprive several regiments of the privilege of beating the *Grenadiers' March*. On this becoming known in London, in January, 1800, the Duke of York at once wrote to Count Woronzow, the Russian ambassador at the Court of St. James's, exculpating the following regiments—namely, the musketeers of General Sedmoratzky, the battalion of Frieksen's grenadiers, the regiment of Fersson's musketeers, the battalions of grenadiers of Majors Ogareff and Mitjucshin, and the regiment of Emmé—which he declared to have evinced much order and bravery in their several encounters with the enemy, and he expressed his regret that they should have undeservedly incurred the Emperor's displeasure.

This letter of the Duke's Count Woronzow at once forwarded it to St. Petersburg, accompanying it by a despatch of his own, in which, besides confirming what the former had stated concerning the good behaviour of the regiments above-mentioned, he recommended to the Emperor's favourable consideration the regiment Sawalshin (late Benkendorff), which, in the battle of the 19th September, had attempted to make up for the loss of one of its own colours by capturing and retaining a standard belonging to the enemy.[10] The Russian troops remained in the Channel Islands until the spring, when they were brought thence, in British transports, and then sent home in their own ships of war which had wintered in English ports.

On their return home, the thanks of Parliament were voted to Vice-Admiral Mitchell, Lieutenant-General Sir Ralph Abercromby, and the officers and men employed under them; and on the 9th January, 1800, the former was invested with the Order of the Bath. The city of London also voted their thanks to the admiral and general, and presented each with a sword valued at 100 guineas. These honours were certainly well deserved, as, although the expedition had failed to accomplish its principal objects, which were for the army to overrun Holland, threaten the French On the Meuse and the Rhine, and, after causing a rising to Belgium, to carry the war into the northern provinces of France, yet the capture of the Dutch fleet at the Helder was achieved, whereby their marine was almost annihilated, the projects of France disconcerted, and the necessity of maintaining a large squadron in the North Sea for the blockade of the Texel obviated.

The principal reasons for the ill-success which subsequently befell it were the extreme tardiness of the first operation, caused by the landing of the troops in successive divisions, and the refusal of the Dutch people, of whose willingness to assist the army great expectations had been entertained, to favour its operations in any way whatever. As for the British public, they completely overlooked the success at the Texel, and clamoured loudly at what they considered the inadequate results of an expedition

---

10. The circumstances attending that loss, according to the reports and general orders, were as follows:—"In the battle of the 8th (19th) that regiment was stationed at the most dangerous point, and suffered considerably more than all the others; but it only lost its colours when the ensign, Schtschegolowitz, during the severest and desperate attack of the enemy, saw that it would be impossible to save them. Encouraged by Ensign Bagogewut, who was with the colours, he tore them off the pole, wrapped them round his body, and thus remained, together with Ensign Bagogewut, on the field of battle. The remaining nine stand of colours belonging to the regiment are all full of holes."—Extract from Count Woronzow's Letter.

which had cost them so dear, both in men and money; and in Parliament, the orators of the Opposition bitterly censured the Ministry, both for the motives which had prompted the expedition and the manner in which it was conducted.

Appendix

No. 1.

List of Russian Ships of War, and of Ships furnished by Great Britain which embarked Russian Troops at Revel.

RUSSIAN.

Ship.	Guns.	Commander.	Corps embarked.	Men.
Alexander Newsky..	74	Rear-Admiral Guhagoff .. Capt. Scott	Sedmoratzky, 1st batt.	949
Gleb	74	„ Demidoff	Emmé Grenadiers	750
Jonas	66	„ Petsoff	Sedmoratzky, 2nd batt., and 50 Hussars	985
January	66	„ Ignatief..........	Arbeneff, 1st batt.	948
Michael	66	„ Pasincoff	Arbeneff, 2nd batt.	936
Panteleymann	66	„ Nolkoffskoi	Ogareff, 1st batt.	739
Ogtheyter....	64	„ Ignatief..........	Chick Grenadiers	739
Venus	54	„ Gasper	Port Osipoff, 1st batt.	539
Raphael	44	„ Boyle	Southoff Riflemen	466
Revel	44	„ Malagen	Timoseff, 1st batt.	739
Constantine .	38	„ Kazencoff		
St. Nicholas ..	38	„ Rose	Artillery, with stores, &c.	240
Neptune, store-ship		„ Dunn............	Detachment Port Osipoff, 1st batt.	200
Minerva, store-ship		„ Ogilvie	Artillery, with stores, &c.	40
				8,270

Ship	Guns	Commander	Corps embarked	Men
Inflexible	64	Capt. S. Ferris	Frieksen's Grenadiers and 20 Hussars	750
Experiment	44	„ Saville	Southoff Riflemen	455
Coromandel	54	„ Mortimer	Benkendorff Grenadiers	800
Dictator	64	„ Hardy	Benkendorff Grenadiers and 58 Hussars	728
Expedition	44	Capt. Sir T. Livingston, Bt.	Benkendorff Grenadiers	403
Diadem	64	„ Dawson	Fersson's Grenadiers (two battalions)	770
Braakel	54	„ Walker		753
Hebe	38	„ Birchall		360
Wassenaar	64	„ Craven	Jereptoff Grenadiers (two battalions)	650
Romulus	36	„ Culverhouse		350
Tromp	54	„ Worseley		650
Alkmaar	56	„ Burdon	Timoseff, 2nd batt.	650
Ulysses	44	„ Pressland	Ogareff, 2nd batt.	
Blonde	32	„ Dobree	The battalion of Mitjucshin, and the remainder of Emmé's regiment, with about 380 convalescents of the first division	730
Niger	32	„ Larmour		
L'Espion	38	„ Rose		
Calcutta	24	„ Anderson		
Walter Boyd, store-ship				
Minerva, store-ship				

8,509

Besides 13 transports, with 2,075 men, 136 horses, and a great quantity of military stores. The whole force embarked, therefore, amounted to nearly 19,000 men. The Russian squadron, under Rear-Admiral Guhagoff sailed from Revel 29th July, and arrived at Elsinore 20th August; sailed again for the Helder 28th August. The squadron under Captain Ferris sailed from Revel 17th August, and arrived at Elsinore 13th September.

The following were the conditions on which the Russian ships and frigates were lent to Great Britain:—

1st. There shall be paid by England, on their quitting the port of Cronstadt in order to proceed to Revel, the port of embarkation, the sum of £58,976. 10s. sterling, as a subsidy for the expenses of equipment, &c., for three months, to be computed from the day of their departure from Cronstadt

2nd. After the expiration of these three months, his Britannic Majesty shall continue the same subsidies—that is to say, of £19,642. 10s sterling a month.

3rd. Independently of this pecuniary succour, his Britannic Majesty shall provide for the subsistence of the crews; and the officers and sailors shall be placed on the same footing as are the English officers and sailors in time of war, and as are the Russian officers and sailors who are at present in the squadron of his Imperial Majesty which is united to the English squadron.

4th. All these stipulations shall have full and entire effect until the return of the above-mentioned ships and frigates into Russian ports.

5th. If it should happen, contrary to all expectations, that these six ships—five frigates and two transport vessels— should not be able, through some unforeseen event, to return to Russia before the close of the present campaign, his Britannic Majesty engages to admit them into English ports, where they shall receive every possible assistance, both for necessary repairs and for the accommodation of the crews and officers.

6th. As the six ships—five frigates and two transport vessels—above-mentioned, having been originally intended for another destination, were furnished with provisions for three months, his Britannic Majesty, instead of furnishing them in kind, as is stated in the 2nd Article, engages to pay, according to an estimate which shall be made, the value of these provisions. With regard to the officers, His Majesty the King of Great Britain will adopt the same principle as has been followed until the present time respecting the officers of the Russian squadron which is joined to the naval forces of England: that shall serve as a rule for indemnifying them for the preparations they have made for the campaign, such as it had been originally intended to take place.

No. 2.

Distribution of the British Army on the 1st September, ·1799.

CAVALRY.

1st Life Guards, London.
2nd ditto, London.
Royal Horse Guards, Swinley Camp.
1st Dragoon Guards, Swinley Camp.
2nd ditto, Swinley Camp.
3rd ditto, Swinley Camp.
4th ditto, ordered from Ireland to Northampton.
5th ditto, Ballinrobe, Ireland.
6th ditto, Ireland.
7th ditto, Worcester.
1st Royal Dragoons, Weymouth.
2nd R. N. British ditto, Dorchester and Barham Downs.
3rd Dragoons, Windsor.
4th ditto, Nottingham.
6th ditto, Uxbridge.
7th Light Dragoons, Swinley Camp, ordered to Holland.
8th ditto, Cape of Good Hope.
9th Dragoons, Carlow, Ireland.
10th Light Dragoons, Staines and Bagshot.
11th ditto, passage to Holland.

12th Light Dragoons, Lisbon.
13th ditto, Birmingham.
14th ditto, Warwick.
15th ditto, Croydon. ordered to Holland.
16th ditto, Swinley Camp.
17th ditto, Swinley Camp.
18th ditto, Holland and Poole.
19th ditto, Trichinopoly, Madras Presidency.
20th (Jamaica Regt.) Lt. Dragoons, Jamaica.
21st Light Dragoons, Bridgenorth.
22nd ditto, Belturbet, Ireland.
23rd ditto, Armagh, Ireland.
24th ditto, Dublin.
25th ditto, Warriore, East Indies.
26th ditto, Lisbon.
27th ditto, East Indies.
28th ditto, Canterbury.
29th ditto, Passage to East Indies.

Foreign Regiments.

Regiment of Mounted Riflemen (Hompesch's), Cashel, Ireland.
The York Hussars, Weymouth.

INFANTRY.

1st Foot Guards—
    1st battalion, London.
    2nd battalion, London.
    3rd battalion, Holland.
Coldstream Guards—
    1st battalion, Holland.
    2nd battalion, London.
3rd Foot Guards—
    1st battalion, Holland.
    2nd battalion, London.
Battalion of Grenadier Companies of the Guards, Holland.
1st Royals—1st batt., Ireland.
    2nd batt., Holland.

24th Regiment, passage home from Canada.
25th ditto, Holland.
26th ditto, St. John's, Canada.
27th ditto, Holland.
28th ditto, Minorca.
29th ditto, Holland.
30th ditto, Messina, Sicily.
31st ditto, ordered to Holland.
32nd ditto, New Providence, Bahamas.
33rd ditto, Madras, E. I.
34th ditto, Hilsea, ordered to Cape.
35th ditto—

2nd (Queen's) Regt., Holland.
3rd (Buffs) ditto, St. Kitt's and Anguilla.
4th (King's) Regiment—
  1st battalion } Ordered to
  2nd battalion } Holland.
  3rd battalion }
5th Regiment—
  1st battalion } Ordered to
  2nd battalion } Holland.
6th Regiment, on passage to Quebec.
7th (Royal Fusiliers), Halifax, N. S.
8th (King's) Regiment, Minorca.
9th Regiment—
  1st battalion } Ordered to
  2nd battalion } Holland.
  3rd battalion, Ashford, Kent.
10th Regiment, Bengal Presidency.
11th ditto, Colchester.
12th ditto, Madras Presidency.
13th ditto, Cashel, Ireland.
14th ditto, Martinique.
15th ditto, Canterbury.
16th ditto, Canterbury.
17th ditto—1st battalion, Holland.
            2nd battalion, Holland.
18th (Royal Irish), Gibraltar.
19th Regiment, Colombo, Ceylon.
20th Regiment—
  1st battalion, Holland.
  2nd battalion, Holland.
21st (Royal Scots Fusiliers), Kilmarnock.
22nd Regiment, Guernsey.
23rd (Royal Welsh Fusiliers), Holland.
  4th battalion, Martinique.
  5th battalion, Surinam.
  6th battalion, Isle of Wight.
  6th ditto, Rifle Company, ordered to Holland.
61st Regiment, Cape of Good Hope.
62nd ditto, Canterbury.
63rd ditto, Holland.
64th ditto, Carrickfergus.
65th ditto, Berwick-on-Tweed.
66th ditto, Nova Scotia.
67th ditto, Jamaica.
68th ditto, Dublin.
69th ditto, Holland.
70th ditto, Gibraltar.
71st (Highland), Stirling.

1st battalion } Ordered to
2nd battalion } Holland.
36th Regiment, Cirencester.
37th ditto, Gibraltar.
38th ditto, Les Saintes, near Guadaloupe.
39th ditto, Demerara and Berbice, Guiana.
40th ditto—1st battalion, Holland.
            2nd battalion, Holland.
41st ditto, Montreal, Canada.
42nd (Highland), Minorca.
43rd Regiment, Jamaica.
44th ditto, Gibraltar.
45th ditto, Dominica.
46th ditto, Barham Downs.
47th ditto, Bermuda.
48th ditto, Gibraltar.
49th ditto, Holland.
50th ditto, Portugal.
51st ditto, Fort St. George, Madras.
52nd ditto, Ashford, Kent.
53rd ditto, St. Vincent's.
54th ditto, Nenagh, Ireland.
55th ditto, Holland.
56th ditto, ordered to Holland.
57th ditto, Trinidad.
58th ditto, Minorca.
59th ditto, Antigua.
60th Royal American Regiment—
  1st battalion, Barbadoes.
  2nd battalion, Montreal, Canada.
  3rd battalion, Tobago.
80th Regiment, Trincomalee, Ceylon.
81st ditto, Cape of Good Hope.
82nd ditto, Canterbury and Blandford.
83rd ditto, Jamaica.
84th ditto, Cape of Good Hope.
85th ditto, Holland.
86th ditto, Bombay Presidency.
87th ditto, Jamaica.
88th ditto, passage to Bombay Presidency.
89th ditto, Minorca.
90th ditto, Minorca.
91st (Highland), Cape of Good Hope.
92nd (ditto), Holland.

72nd (ditto), Perth.
73rd (ditto), field service, Mysore.
74th (ditto), Wallajabad, E. I.
75th (ditto), field service, Mysore.
76th Regiment, Dinapore, Bengal.
77th ditto, Cochin, East Indies.
78th (Highland), Bengal Presidency.
79th (ditto), Holland.

Scotch Brigade, Madras Presidency.
New South Wales Corps, New South Wales.
Queen's Rangers, Upper Canada.
Minorca Regiment, Minorca.
Villette's ditto }
Brodrick's ditto } both raising.
Royal Garrison Battalion, Jersey.
Royal Waggon Train, raising.

Companies of Invalids—Five at Alderney, three at Berwick, one at Chatham, two at Chester, nine at Guernsey, two at Hull, eleven at Jersey, one at Languard Fort, four in North Britain, six at Plymouth, one at Pendennis Castle, Falmouth, four at Portsmouth, one in Scilly Isles, three at Sheerness, one at Tilbury Fort, and six in Ireland.

1st West India Regiment, St. Lucia.
2nd ditto, Grenada.
3rd ditto, St. Pierre.
4th ditto, St. Vincent's.
5th ditto, Jamaica.
6th ditto, Honduras.

7th West India Regiment, Prince Rupert's, Dominica.
8th ditto, Prince Rupert's, Dominica.
9th ditto, Leeward Islands.
10th ditto, Leeward Islands.
11th ditto, Demerara.
12th ditto, Leeward Islands.

ROYAL REGIMENT OF ARTILLERY.

Horse Artillery—One troop each in Holland, and at Brighton, Canterbury, Woodbridge, Poole, and Woolwich—in all, six troops, each consisting of 2 staff sergeants, 3 sergeants, 3 corporals, 7 bombardiers, 1 trumpeter, 2 collar makers, 1 wheelwright, 1 carriage-smith, 4 farriers, 97 gunners, and 71 drivers.

Foot Artillery—Six battalions, each consisting of 2 staff sergeants, 40 sergeants, 40 corporals, 70 bombardiers, 30 drummers, and 980 gunners.

1st battalion—Leeward Islands, Jamaica, Cape of Good Hope, Gibraltar, Portsmouth, Purfleet, Colchester, Plymouth, Guernsey, and Woolwich.

2nd battalion — Newfoundland, New Brunswick, Halifax, N. S. ; Jamaica, Gibraltar, Minorca, and Woolwich.

3rd battalion—Martinique, Holland, Canterbury, and Woolwich.

4th battalion—Quebec, Cape of Good Hope, Martinique, Minorca, Gibraltar, Ringmer, Plymouth, Leith, Jersey, Holland, and Woolwich.

5th battalion—Ireland, Plymouth, Canterbury, Newcastle, Gibraltar, Portsmouth, Perth, and Woolwich.

6th battalion (formed this year of six new companies and two companies lately forming an East India detachment)—Cape of Good Hope and Woolwich.

No. 3

Return of Killed, Wounded, and Missing, of the British Forces under the command of General Sir Ralph Abercromby, K.B., in the Action of the Helder, 29th August, 1799.

General Staff—1 lieutenant-general, 1 colonel, 1 lieutenant-colonel, 1 captain, wounded.

Detachment of Royal Engineers—1 lieutenant-colonel killed; 2 subalterns wounded.

1st Brigade.

Staff—1 lieutenant-colonel killed.

Grenadier Battalion of the Guards—1 serjeant, 2 rank and file, killed; 1 captain, 2 serjeants, 48 rank and file, wounded; 1 rank and file missing.

3rd Battalion 1st Guards—1 captain, 13 rank and file, wounded.

2nd Brigade.

1st Battalion Coldstream Guards—7 rank and file wounded; 1 rank and file missing.

3rd Brigade.

Staff—1 captain wounded.

2nd (or Queen's) Regiment—2 rank and file killed; 1 subaltern, 1 serjeant, 21 rank and file, wounded; 1 rank and file missing.

27th Regiment—1 subaltern, 1 serjeant, 6 rank and file, killed; 1 lieutenant-colonel, 1 serjeant, 43 rank and file, wounded; 7 rank and file missing.

29th Regiment—3 rank and file killed; 1 captain, 1 subaltern, 3 serjeants, 1 drummer, 30 rank and file, wounded.

69th Regiment—1 serjeant, 13 rank and file, wounded.

85th Regiment—8 rank and file killed; 1 major, 1 captain, 2 subalterns, 29 rank and file, wounded; 16 rank and file missing.

Reserve.

23rd Royal Welsh Fusiliers—18 rank and file killed; 3 captains, 5 serjeants, 69 rank and file, wounded.

55th Regiment—1 serjeant, 12 rank and file, killed; 1 colonel, 2 captains, 5 serjeants, 61 rank and file, wounded.

Total.

Killed—2 lieutenant-colonels, 1 subaltern, 3 serjeants, 51 rank and file. Wounded—1 lieutenant-general, 2 colonels, 2 lieutenant-colonels, 1 major, 11 captains, 6 subalterns, 18 serjeants, 1 drummer, 334 rank and file. Missing—26 rank and file. There were also drowned in landing—1 non-commissioned officer and 4 gunners, Royal Artillery, and 1 serjeant and 14 rank and file of the 92nd Highlanders.

Nominal Return of Officers Killed and Wounded.

General and Brigade Staff—Lieutenant-Colonel Smollet, 1st Guards, Brigade-Major of 1st brigade, killed. Lieutenant-General Sir James Pulteney, Bart., second in command; Colonel Hon. John Hope, 25th regiment, Deputy Adjutant-General; Lieutenant-Colonel Murray, 3rd

Guards, Assistant Quarter-Master-General ; Captain Arthur M'Donald, 5th West India regiment, Assistant Quarter-Master-General ; Captain Manners, 82nd regiment, Aide-de-camp to Major-General Coote; wounded.

Royal Engineers—Lieutenant-Colonel Hay, killed; Lieutenants Chapman and Squire, wounded.

Grenadier Battalion of the Guards—Captain Gunthorpe, 1st Guards, wounded.

3rd Battalion 1st Guards—Captain Ruddock, wounded.

2nd (or Queen's) Regiment—Lieutenant Swan, wounded.

27th Regiment—Lieutenant Crow, killed; Lieutenant-Colonel Graham, wounded.

29th Regiment—Captain Wyatt and Lieutenant Grove, wounded.

85th Regiment—Captain McIntosh, Lieutenants Travers and Berry, Major Otley, wounded.

23rd Royal Welsh Fusiliers—Captains Berry, Ellis, and Hon. G. M'Donald, wounded.

55th Regiment—Colonel M'Donald, Captains Brown and Power, Volunteer John M'Gregor, wounded.

No. 4.

Return of Volunteers given by the Embodied Militia to the Regular Army, between the 18th July and 15th November, 1799.

Royal Artillery	344	31st Regiment	.	955
1st Foot Guards	454	35th ,,	. .	1,764
2nd ,,	557	36th ,,	. .	769
3rd ,,	290	40th ,,	. .	1,504
4th Regiment .	3,034	46th ,,	. .	694
5th ,,	1,268	52nd ,,	. .	1,861
9th ,,	2,695	56th ,,	. .	774
15th ,,	1,548	62nd ,,	. .	1,043
16th ,,	761	63rd ,,	. .	755
17th ,,	1,558	82nd ,,	. .	702
20th ,,	1,647			
		Total		24,977

No. 5.

Isis, under sail, in line-of-battle,

August 30th.

Sir—I desire you will instantly hoist the flag of His Serene Highness the Prince of Orange. If you do, you will be immediately considered friends of the King of Great Britain, my most gracious sovereign; otherwise, take the consequences. Painful it will be to me for the loss of blood it may occasion, but the guilt will be on your own head.

I have the honour to be, Sir,

Your most obedient humble servant,

(Signed) Andrew Mitchell,

Vice-Admiral and Commander-in-Chief

of His Majesty's ships employed

in the present Expedition,

To Rear-Admiral Storey or the Commander-
in-Chief of the Dutch Squadron.

Rear-Admiral Storey to Vice-Admiral Mitchell

On board the *Washington*,

anchored under the Vleiter, 30th August.

Admiral—Neither your superiority, nor the threat that the spilling of human blood should be laid to my account, could prevent my showing you to the last moment what I could do for my sovereign, whom I acknowledge to be no other than the Batavian people and its representatives, when your Princess and the Orange flags have obtained their end.

The traitors whom I commanded refused to fight; and nothing remains to me and my brave officers, but vain rage and the dreadful reflection of our present situation: I therefore deliver over to you the fleet which I commanded. From this moment it is your obligation to provide for the safety of my officers, and the few brave men who are on board the Batavian ships, as I declare myself and my officers prisoners of war, and remain to be considered as such.

I am, with respect,

S. Storey.

To Admiral Mitchell, commanding his Britannic Majesty's Squadron in the Texel.

Proclamation issued by Vice-Admiral Mitchell, on the occasion of the surrender of the Dutch Fleet,

Isis, August 30th.

The undersigned, Vice-Admiral in the service of His Majesty the King of Great Britain, charged with the execution of the naval part of the expedition to restore the *Stadtholder* and the old and lawful constitution of the Seven United Provinces, guaranteed by His Majesty, having agreed that, in consequence of the summons to Rear-Admiral Storey, the ships, after hoisting the ancient colours, will be considered as in the service of the allies of the British Crown, and under the orders of His Serene Highness the Hereditary *Stadtholder*, Captain and Admiral-General of the Seven United Provinces, has thought it proper to give an account of this agreement to the brave crews of the different ships, and to summon them by the same to behave in a peaceable and orderly manner, so that no complaints may be represented by the officer the undersigned will send on board each of the ships, to keep proper order, until the intentions of His Majesty and His Serene Highness the Prince of Orange, as Admiral-General, shall be known for the farther destination of these ships, on account of which dispatches will be immediately sent off. And to make them aware that, in case their conduct should not be so (such ?) as may be expected from the known loyalty and attachment of the Dutch navy to the illustrious House of Orange, on this occasion, any excess or irregularity will be punished with the severity which the disorders that may have been committed merit

(Signed)   Andrew Mitchell.

No. 6.

List of Ships of War remaining of the Batavian Navy after the capture of their Fleet at the Helder, in August, 1799.

At Amsterdam:—
  Avenger, 76.
  Admiral Zoutman, 76.
  Chatham, 76.
  Bato, 76.
  Shrick Verwekker, 68.
  Kersteller, 68.
At Flushing:—
  Pluto, 68.
In Norway:—
  Pollux, 44.
  Jaager, 36.
  Picstic, 24.
  Iris, 16.
  Flying Fish, 14.

In the Meuse:—
  Brutus, 76.
  Oldan Barnivelt, 68.
  Neptunus, 68.
  Revolution, 68.
  Doggerbank, 68.
  Pictor Paulus, 68.
  Karlenaar, 68.
  John de Witt, 68.
  De Endracht, 44.
  Juno, 36.
  Phœnix, 36.
  Scipio, 24.

Also, the following brigs at various stations:—Hippomenes, 18; Ajax, 18; Daphne, 18; Atalante, 18; Spy, 16; and Echo, 16.

No. 7.

Return of Killed, Wounded, and Missing, of the British Army under the command of Lieutenant-General Sir Ralph Abercromby, K.B., in the Action of the Zuype, 10th September, 1799.

General and Brigade Staff—1 major-general, 1 captain, wounded.

Royal Artillery—3 rank and file killed; 1 subaltern, 1 serjeant, 6 rank and file, wounded.

Grenadier Battalion of the Guards—6 rank and file killed; 1 captain, 1 serjeant, 13 rank and file, wounded.

3rd Battalion 1st Guards—5 rank and file wounded.

1st Battalion Coldstream Guards—1 rank and file killed; 8 rank and file wounded.

1st Battalion 3rd Guards—2 rank and file killed; 1 captain, 3 rank and file, wounded.

85th Regiment—1 rank and file killed; 3 rank and file wounded.

2nd Battalion 1st Royal Regiment—1 subaltern, 3 rank and file, wounded.

92nd Regiment—1 rank and file killed; 1 captain, 3 rank and file, wounded.

1st Battalion 17th Regiment—2 rank and file killed.

2nd Battalion 17th Regiment—2 rank and file killed; 18 rank and file wounded.

1st Battalion 40th Regiment—1 rank and file killed; 10 rank and file wounded.

1st Battalion 20th Regiment—14 rank and file killed; 1 lieutenant-colonel, 1 major, 4 subalterns, 25 rank and file, wounded; 14 rank and file missing.

2nd Battalion 20th Regiment—4 rank and file killed; 1 captain, 1 serjeant, 34 rank and file, wounded; 1 serjeant, 4 rank and file, missing.

Total—37 rank and file killed; 1 major-general, 1 lieutenant-colonel, 1 major, 5 captains, 6 subalterns, 2 serjeants, 131 rank and file, wounded; 1 serjeant, 18 rank and file, missing.

NOMINAL RETURN OF OFFICERS WOUNDED.

General and Brigade Staff—Major-General Moore, commanding 4th Brigade; Captain Halket, 76th Regiment, Aide-de-camp to Lieutenant-General Sir Ralph Abercromby.

Royal Artillery—Lieutenant Simpson.

Grenadier Battalion of Guards—Captain Neville, 3rd Guards.

1st Battalion 3rd Guards—Captain Neville.

2nd Battalion 1st Royals—Lieutenant Gordon.

92nd Highlanders—Captain Hon. John Ramsay.

1st Battalion 20th Regiment — Lieutenant-Colonel George Smith, Major Ross, Lieutenants Colborne, Charles Des Vœux, and Christopher Hamilton, and Lieutenant and Adjutant Samuel South.

2nd Battalion 20th Regiment — Captain-Lieutenant L. Ferdinand Adams.

No. 8.

Return of Killed, Wounded, and Missing of the British Army under the command of His Royal Highness the Duke of York, in the Action of the 19th September, 1799.

11th Light Dragoons—1 rank and file wounded.

Royal Artillery—12 rank and file killed; 1 subaltern, 18 rank and file, wounded; 16 rank and file missing.

Grenadier Battalion of the Guards—1 lieutenant-colonel, 1 captain, 11 rank and file, killed; 1 lieutenant-colonel, 1 captain, 2 serjeants, 44 rank and file, wounded; 4 serjeants, 23 rank and file, missing.

3rd Battalion 1st Regiment of Guards—2 rank and file killed; 2 lieutenant-colonels, 2 captains, 1 subaltern, 2 serjeants, 42 rank and file, wounded; 43 rank and file missing.

1st Battalion Coldstream Regiment of Guards—1 serjeant, 9 rank and file, killed; 1 lieutenant-colonel, 1 serjeant, 21 rank and file, wounded; 1 serjeant, 13 rank and file, missing.

1st Battalion 3rd Regiment of Guards—2 rank and file killed; 1 serjeant, 1 drummer, 17 rank and file, wounded.

27th Regiment of Foot—1 rank and file wounded.

1st Battalion 17th Regiment of Foot—6 rank and file killed; 2 majors, 2 captains, 2 subalterns, 2 serjeants, 34 rank and file, wounded; 3 rank and file missing.

2nd Battalion ditto—10 rank and file killed; 1 major, 1 subaltern, 4 serjeants, 19 rank and file, wounded.

1st Battalion 40th Regiment of Foot—1 subaltern, 16 rank and file, killed ; 1 major, 4 captains, 1 subaltern, 2 serjeants, 47 rank and file, wounded; 1 captain, 12 rank and file, missing.

2nd Battalion ditto—10 rank and file killed; 3 captains, 1 subaltern, 4 serjeants, 39 rank and file, wounded; 11 rank and file missing.

1st Battalion 5th Regiment of Foot—5 rank and file killed; 1 lieutenant-colonel, 1 subaltern, 2 serjeants, 1 drummer, 1 rank and file, wounded; 2 serjeants, 1 drummer, 1 rank and file, missing.

1st Battalion 35th Regiment of Foot—1 lieutenant-colonel, 2 majors, 1 captain, 3 subalterns, wounded; 2 serjeants, 1 drummer, missing. N.B.—350 rank and file of this regiment could not exactly be accounted for when the general return of loss was made up, owing to the nature of the action, and the regiment having been sent at its close to the Helder, in charge of prisoners; but nearly 100 were supposed to have been killed, and the remainder wounded and missing.

1st Battalion 9th Regiment of Foot—1 subaltern, 1 staff, killed; 3 subalterns wounded; 10 serjeants, 1 drummer, 203 rank and file, missing.

2nd Battalion ditto—1 captain, 1 serjeant, 16 rank and file, killed; 1 lieutenant-colonel, 1 subaltern, 4 serjeants, 46 rank and file, wounded; 1 serjeant, 97 rank and file, missing.

56th Regiment of Foot—30 rank and file killed; 2 captains, 1 subaltern, 33 rank and file, wounded; 2 serjeants, 2 drummers, 57 rank and file, missing.

Royal Navy (crews of gunboats)—4 seamen killed; 1 lieutenant and 7 seamen wounded.

Total (exclusive of 35th Regiment)—1 lieutenant-colonel, 2 captains, 2 subalterns, 1 staff, 2 serjeants, 121 rank and file, 4 seamen, killed; 6 lieutenant-colonels, 4 majors, 15 captains, 13 subalterns, 20 serjeants, 2 drummers, 364 rank and file, 7 seamen, wounded; 20 serjeants, 4 drummers, 479 rank and file, missing.

NOMINAL RETURN OF OFFICERS KILLED, WOUNDED, AND MISSING.

Royal Artillery—First Lieutenant Eligie wounded and taken prisoner; Volunteer John Douglas wounded.

Grenadier Battalion of Guards—Lieutenant-Colonel Morris, Coldstream Guards, and Captain Gunthorpe, 1st Guards, killed; Colonel Wynyard, 1st Foot Guards, and Captain Neville, 3rd Foot Guards, wounded.

3rd Battalion 1st Guards—Lieutenant-Colonel Cook wounded; Lieutenant-Colonel Dawkins and Captain Forbes wounded and taken prisoners; Captain Henry Wheatley wounded; Ensign D'Oyley wounded and taken prisoner.

1st Battalion Coldstream Guards — Lieutenant-Colonel Cunningham wounded.

1st Battalion 17th Regiment—Majors Grey and Cockburne, Captains Grace and Knight, wounded; Lieutenant Wickham missing; Lieutenant Wilson and Ensign Thomson wounded.

2nd Battalion 17th Regiment—Major Wood and Lieutenant Saunders wounded.

1st Battalion 40th Regiment—Ensign Elcomb killed; Major Wingfield, Captains Dancer, Thompson, Gear, Myers, and Lieutenant Williams, wounded; Captain O'Donnell missing.

2nd Battalion 40th Regiment — Captain Trollope mortally wounded; Captains Dancer and Thornton, and Lieutenant M'Pherson, wounded.

1st Battalion 5th Regiment—Lieutenant-Colonel Stephenson wounded; Lieutenant Harris mortally wounded.

1st Battalion 35th Regiment—Lieutenant-Colonel Oswald and Major Hay wounded; Major Petit wounded and taken prisoner; Captain Manary, Ensigns Wilkinson, Dean, and Jones, wounded.

1st Battalion 9th Regiment—Lieutenant Woodford and Quartermaster Holles killed; Lieutenant Smith wounded and taken prisoner; Lieutenants Grant and Rothwell wounded.

2nd Battalion 9th Regiment—Captain Balfour killed; Lieutenant-Colonel Crew wounded; Ensign French wounded and taken prisoner; Ensign Butler missing.

56th Regiment—Captains King and Gilman, and Lieutenant Prater, wounded.

Royal Navy—Lieutenant Rowad wounded.

No. 9.

Return of Killed, Wounded, and Missing, of the British Army under the command of His Royal Highness the Duke of York, in the Battle of Bergen, 2nd October, 1799.

CAVALRY BRIGADE.

Staff—1 major wounded.

7th (or Queen's Own) Light Dragoons—2 rank and file, 4 horses, killed; 11 rank and file, 25 horses, wounded; 1 horse missing.

11th Light Dragoons—1 rank and file, 2 horses, killed; 4 rank and file, 4 horses, wounded.

15th (or King's) Light Dragoons—2 rank and file, 4 horses, killed; 1 lieutenant-colonel, 9 rank and file, 3 horses, wounded; 2 horses missing.

Royal Artillery—9 rank and file, 34 horses, killed; 1 captain, 4 serjeants, 61 rank and file, 46 horses, wounded.

1ST INFANTRY BRIGADE.

Grenadier Battalion of Guards—1 rank and file killed; 1 serjeant, 18 rank and file, wounded.

3rd Battalion 1st Guards—6 rank and file killed; 1 major, 2 subalterns, 5 serjeants, 47 rank and file, wounded; 8 rank and file missing.

3RD INFANTRY BRIGADE.

Staff—1 captain wounded.

2nd (or Queen's) Regiment—2 rank and file killed; 2 serjeants, 1 drummer, 13 rank and file, wounded; 2 rank and file missing.

27th Regiment—4 rank and file killed; 1 captain, 3 subalterns, 1 drummer, 40 rank and file, wounded; 1 rank and file missing.

29th Regiment—1 serjeant, 7 rank and file, killed; 1 captain, 3 subalterns, 1 serjeant, 30 rank and file, wounded; 1 serjeant, 10 rank and file, missing.

85th Regiment—1 subaltern, 6 rank and file, killed; 1 lieutenant-colonel, 2 captains, 1 subaltern, 1 serjeant, 66 rank and file, wounded; 9 rank and file missing.

Staff—1 major-general wounded.

2nd Battalion 1st Royal Regiment—7 rank and file killed; 2 captains, 5 subalterns, 4 serjeants, 61 rank and file, wounded; 10 rank and file missing.

25th Regiment—1 captain, 1 subaltern, 2 serjeants, 32 rank and file, killed; 1 major, 3 captains, 2 serjeants, 61 rank and file, wounded; 13 rank and file missing.

49th Regiment—1 captain, 1 subaltern, 1 serjeant, 30 rank and file, killed; 1 major, 2 captains, 2 subalterns, 3 serjeants, 50 rank and file, wounded; 1 subaltern, 3 serjeants, 1 drummer, 21 rank and file, missing.

79th Regiment—1 captain, 13 rank and file, killed; 1 colonel, 3 subalterns, 4 serjeants, 45 rank and file, wounded; 2 rank and file missing.

92nd Regiment—1 captain, 2 subalterns, 3 serjeants, 54 rank and file, killed; 1 colonel, 4 captains, 6 subalterns, 6 serjeants, 1 drummer, 175 rank and file, wounded; 39 rank and file missing.

5TH INFANTRY BRIGADE.

2nd Battalion 17th Regiment—2 rank and file killed; 2 subalterns, 5 rank and file, wounded.

1st Battalion 40th Regiment—1 serjeant, 2 rank and file, wounded.

2nd ditto   ditto   —1 staff wounded.

6TH INFANTRY BRIGADE.

1st Battalion 20th Regiment—1 captain, 1 serjeant, 9 rank and file, wounded; 1 rank and file missing.

2nd Battalion 20th Regiment—3 rank and file killed; 1 subaltern, 29 rank and file, wounded; 3 rank and file missing.

63rd Regiment—1 rank and file killed; 1 captain, 2 subalterns, 3 serjeants, 33 rank and file, wounded; 2 rank and file missing.

7TH INFANTRY BRIGADE.

1st Battalion 4th Regiment—1 rank and file killed; 1 subaltern, 3 rank and file, wounded; 1 rank and file missing.

2nd Battalion 4th Regiment—1 rank and file killed; 1 serjeant, 4 rank and file, wounded; 1 serjeant, 1 rank and file, missing.

3rd Battalion 34th Regiment—1 rank and file killed, 1 rank and file wounded, 4 rank and file missing.

31st Regiment—2 rank and file killed; 1 subaltern, 6 rank and file, wounded; 5 rank and file missing.

RESERVE.

Grenadier Battalion of the Line—4 serjeants, 9 rank and file, killed; 2 captains, 3 serjeants, 59 rank and file, wounded; 1 captain, 2 subalterns, 2 serjeants, 2 drummers, 30 rank and file, wounded.

Light Infantry Battalion of the Line—4 rank and file killed; 2 captains, 2 serjeants, 57 rank and file, wounded; 5 rank and file missing.

23rd Royal Welch Fusiliers—7 rank and file killed; 2 subalterns, 1 serjeant, 3 drummers, 49 rank and file, wounded; 7 rank and file missing.

55th Regiment—1 major, 2 rank and file, killed; 1 subaltern, 1 serjeant, 1 drummer, 16 rank and file, wounded.

Rifle Company 6th Battalion 60th Regiment— 6 rank and file killed, 7 rank and file wounded, 4 rank and file missing.

1 major, 5 captains, 5 subalterns, 11 serjeants, 215 rank and file, 44 horses, killed; 1 major-general, 2 colonels, 2 lieutenant-colonels, 4 majors, 23 captains, 39 subalterns, 1 staff, 46 serjeants, 7 drummers, 980 rank and file, 78 horses, wounded; 1 captain, 4 subalterns, 7 serjeants, 3 drummers, 178 rank and file, missing.

NOMINAL RETURN OF OFFICERS KILLED, WOUNDED, AND MISSING.

Staff—Major-General Moore, commanding 4th Brigade; Lieutenant-Colonel Sontag, Military Commissary to the troops forming under the Prince of Orange; Major Calcraft, 25th Light Dragoons, Aide-de-Camp to Colonel Lord Paget; Captain W. Gray, 2nd (Queen's) Regiment, Brigade-Major of the 3rd Brigade; Lieutenant Jackson, 40th Regiment, acting on the Staff with the Russian army, wounded.

15th Light Dragoons—Lieutenant-Colonel Erskine, wounded.

Royal Artillery—Captain Nichol, (mortally) wounded.

27th Regiment—Captain M'Murdo, Lieutenant and Adjutant Tuthill, Ensign and Quartermaster Ryan, Ensign Brazier, wounded.

29th Regiment—Captain White, Lieutenants Tandy, Rowan, and Bamfield, wounded.

85th Regiment—Lieutenant Nestor, killed; Lieutenant-Colonel Ross, Captains Bowen and M'Intosh, Lieutenant Reilly, wounded.

2nd Battalion 1st Royals—Captains Barnes and Hunter, Lieutenants Ainslie, Frazer, Edmonstown, and Patton, Ensign Birmingham, wounded; Lieutenant Hope, wounded and taken prisoner.

25th Regiment—Captain-Lieutenant Johnston, Lieutenant M'Donald, killed; Major Hinde, Captains Callander, Scott, and Carew, Lieutenants Light, Grant, Peat, and Austin, wounded.

49th Regiment—Captain Archer, Ensign Ginn, killed; Major Hutchinson, Captains Sharp and Robins, Lieutenant Urquhart, and Ensign Hill, wounded; Lieutenant Johnson, missing.

79th Regiment—Captain James Campbell, killed; Colonel Alan Cameron, Lieutenants M'Donald, M'Neil, and Rose, wounded.

92nd Regiment—Captain William M'Intosh, Lieutenants Alexander Fraser and Gordon M'Hardy, killed; Colonel Marquis of Huntly, Captains John Cameron, Alexander Gordon, and Peter Grant, Lieutenants G. Frazer, Charles Chad, and Donald M'Donald, Ensigns Charles Cameron, John M'Pherson and James Bent, wounded; Captain John M'Lean, wounded and taken prisoner.

2nd Battalion 17th Regiment—Lieutenants Wynne and Morrison, wounded.

2nd Battalion 40th Regiment—Quartermaster Philips, wounded.

1st Battalion 20th Regiment—Captain Pawlett, wounded.

2nd Battalion   ditto   —Ensign Mills, wounded.

63rd Regiment—Captain M'Niver, Lieutenant Le Geyte, Ensign Hall, wounded.

1st Battalion 4th Regiment—Ensign Carruthers, wounded.

31st Regiment—Ensign King, wounded.

Grenadier Battalion of the Line—Captains Leith (31st Regiment) and Pratt (5th Regiment), Lieutenants Stafford (31st Regiment) and Philpot (35th Regiment), and Volunteer Barrington, wounded; Captain O'Neil, (56th Regiment), wounded and missing.

Light Infantry Battalion of the Line—Captains Robertson (35th Regiment) and Hitchman (3rd Battalion 4th Regiment), wounded.

23rd Royal Welch Fusiliers—Lieutenants A. M'Lean and William Keith, wounded.

55th Regiment—Major William Lumsden, killed; Lieutenant Dixon, wounded.

Return of Killed, Wounded, and Missing, of the Russian Forces under the command of His Royal Highness the Duke of York, in the Battle of Bergen, 2nd October, 1799.

	General Officers.	Field Officers and Captains.	Subalterns.	N. C. Officers.	Privates.	Horses.
Killed or missing..	..	1	3	9	159	50
Wounded	1	1	18	38	365	..
Total	1	2	21	47	524	50

No. 10

General Order issued by the Duke of York after the Battle of Bergen, 2nd October, 1799.

Head-Quarters at Alkmaar, Oct, 5th.

Parole—*Alkmaar;* Countersign—*St George.*

His Royal Highness the Commander-in-Chief desires to express to the army his warmest thanks for the steady and persevering gallantry of their conduct in the general action of the 2nd instant, to which alone is to be ascribed the complete victory gained over the enemy, under circumstances of the greatest difficulty.

His Royal Highness feels it particularly incumbent on him to offer his best thanks to General Sir Ralph Abercromby, Lieutenant-General Dundas, and Major-General Emmé, who commanded and led the right, centre, and left divisions of the army to the attack; as also to Lieutenant-General Hulse, for the assistance he afforded to Sir Ralph Abercromby; and thinks it no less his duty to place on record the names of the following general officers and brigades of British, who had an opportunity of contributing to the success of that ever memorable and distinguished day:—

1st. Colonel Lord Paget, commanding the British cavalry,

consisting of the 7th, 11th, and 15th Regiments of Light Dragoons.

2nd. Major-General D'Oyley's brigade, consisting of Grenadiers of the Guards and 3rd battalion 1st Regiment of Guards.

3rd. Major-General Burrard's brigade, consisting of 1st battalion Coldstream Guards and 1st battalion 3rd Regiment of Guards.

4th. Major-General Coote's brigade, consisting of 2nd (or Queen's), 27th, 29th, and 85th Regiments of Foot

5th. Major-General Moore's brigade, consisting of 2nd battalion of the Royals, 25th, 49th, 79th, and 92nd Regiments.

6th. Major-General Hutchinson's brigade, consisting of 1st and 2nd battalions 20th Regiment, and 63rd Regiment.

7th. Major-General Lord Chatham's brigade, consisting of the 1st, 2nd, and 3rd battalions 4th Regiment, and 31st Regiment

8th. Colonel Macdonald, commanding the Grenadiers of the Line, the Light Infantry of the Line, and the 23rd and 55th Regiments of Foot.

9th. Major-General Knox, attached during the day to the Russian column, and afterwards sent, in consequence of Major-General Moore's being wounded to take command of his brigade.

His Royal Highness likewise desires to express his satisfaction at the conduct of Lieutenant-Colonel Whitworth and Major Judson, attached to General Sir Ralph Abercromby's column, and also to Lieutenant-Colonel Smith, commanding the artillery of the wing under Lieutenant-General Dundas.

No. 11.

Return of Killed, Wounded, and Missing of the British Army under the command of His Royal Highness the Duke of York in the Battle of Egmont, 6th October, 1799.

CAVALRY BRIGADE.

7th Light Dragoons—2 rank and file, 2 horses, killed; 7 rank and file, 6 horses, wounded; 2 rank and file, 1 horse, missing.

11th Light Dragoons—1 serjeant, 7 rank and file, 7 horses, killed; 18 rank and file, 13 horses, wounded; 7 rank and file, 7 horses, missing.

15th Light Dragoons—2 rank and file, 1 horse, wounded.

Royal Artillery—1 rank and file killed, 1 rank and file wounded.

1ST INFANTRY BRIGADE.

Grenadier Battalion of the Guards—1 rank and file killed, 18 rank and file wounded.

3rd Battalion 1st Guards—3 rank and file killed; 1 colonel, 1 subaltern, 26 rank and file, wounded; 1 lieutenant-colonel, 21 rank and file, missing.

2ND INFANTRY BRIGADE.

1st Battalion Coldstream Guards—1 rank and file killed, 13 rank and file wounded, 3 rank and file missing.

1st Battalion 3rd Guards—1 serjeant, 4 rank and file, killed; 1 staff, 2 serjeants, 17 rank and file, wounded.

3RD INFANTRY BRIGADE.

2nd (or Queen's) Regiment—1 rank and file wounded, 8 rank and file missing.

27th Regiment—17 rank and file missing.

85th Regiment—25 rank and file missing.

5TH INFANTRY BRIGADE.

1st Battalion 40th Regiment—30 rank and file missing.

6TH INFANTRY BRIGADE.

1st Battalion 20th Regiment—1 lieutenant-colonel, 1 subaltern, 7 rank and file, killed; 1 major, 1 captain, 3 subalterns, 2 serjeants, 47 rank and file, wounded; 9 rank and file missing.

2nd Battalion 20th Regiment—7 rank and file killed; 3 captains, 1 subaltern, 67 rank and file, wounded; 1 serjeant, 1 drummer, 30 rank and file, missing.

63rd Regiment—1 serjeant, 1 drummer, 8 rank and file, killed; 1 captain, 4 subalterns, 4 serjeants, 140 rank and file, wounded; 45 rank and file missing.

7TH INFANTRY BRIGADE.

1st Battalion 4th Regiment—15 rank and file killed; 1 lieutenant-colonel, 3 subalterns, 2 serjeants, 39 rank and file, wounded; 19 rank and file missing.

2nd Battalion 4th Regiment—1 lieutenant-colonel, 2 rank and file, killed; 2 captains, 4 subalterns, 1 serjeant, 35 rank and file, wounded; 1 lieutenant-colonel, 1 major, 4 captains, 10 subalterns, and 169 rank and file, missing.

3rd Battalion 4th Regiment—2 rank and file killed; 2 majors, 1 serjeant, 34 rank and file, wounded; 1 captain, 1 subaltern, 4 serjeants, 1 drummer, 141 rank and file, missing.

31st Regiment—1 subaltern, 10 rank and file, killed; 3 subalterns, 4 serjeants, 82 rank and file, wounded; 33 rank and file missing.

Reserve.

Grenadier Battalion of the Line—4 rank and file killed; 2 subalterns, 1 serjeant, 49 rank and file, wounded; 10 rank and file missing

Light Infantry Battalion of the Line—5 rank and file killed; 3 subalterns, 3 serjeants, 34 rank and file, wounded; 9 rank and file missing.

23rd Royal Welsh Fusiliers—6 rank and file killed; 1 serjeant, 35 rank and file, wounded.

55th Regiment—2 serjeants, 10 rank and file, wounded.

Total.

Killed, 2 lieutenant-colonels, 2 subalterns, 3 serjeants, 1 drummer, 85 rank and file, and 9 horses; wounded, 1 colonel, 1 lieutenant-colonel, 3 majors, 7 captains, 23 subalterns, 1 staff, 23 serjeants, 675 rank and file, and 20 horses; missing, 2 lieutenant-colonels, 1 major, 5 captains, 11 subalterns, 13 serjeants, 2 drummers, 578 rank and file, and 8 horses.

Nominal Return of Officers Killed, Wounded, and Missing.

3rd Battalion 1st Guards—Wounded, Colonel Maitland and Ensign Burke; missing, Lieutenant-Colonel Lake.

1st Battalion 3rd Guards—Wounded, Surgeon Babington.

1st Battalion 20th Regiment—Killed, Lieutenant-Colonel Philip Bainbridge and Ensign McCurtis; wounded, Major Campbell, Captain Newman, Lieutenant Stevens, and Ensigns Fevel and Humphries.

2nd Battalion 20th Regiment—Wounded, Captains Masters, Wallace, and Torrens, and Ensign Drury.

63rd Regiment—Wounded, Captain-Lieutenant Wardlaw, Lieutenants Bennet, Purcell, Sankey, and McIntosh.

1st Battalion 4th Regiment—Wounded, Lieutenant-Colonel Hodgson, Ensigns Johnston, Carruthers, and Nicholls.

2nd Battalion 4th Regiment—Killed, Lieutenant-Colonel Dickson; wounded, Captains Gilman and Palman, Lieutenants Deare and Wilson, Ensigns Highmore and Archibald; missing, Lieutenant-Colonel Cholmondeley, Major Pringle, Captains Archdail, Brodie, Gilmore, and Chaplin, Lieutenants Gazeley, Wilson, Deare, and Wilbraham, Ensigns Brown, Hill, Ellis, Anderson, McPherson, and Tryon.

3rd Battalion 4th Regiment—Killed, Lieutenant Forster; wounded, Majors Wynch and Horndon; missing, Captain Williamson, Ensign Algeo.

31st Regiment—Wounded, Ensigns Williams, Johnston, and King.

Return of Killed, Wounded, and Missing of the Russian Forces under the command of His Royal Highness the Duke of York, in the Battle of Egmont, 6th October, 1799.

	Field Officers and Captains.	Subalterns.	Non-Com. Officers.	Privates.
Killed or taken prisoners.. ..		8	15	359
Wounded..............	5	21	34	675
Total..........	5	29	49	1,034

No. 12.

Return of Killed, Wounded, and Missing of the British Army under the command of His Royal Highness the Duke of York, between the 6th and 10th of October.

18th Light Dragoons—15 horses killed; 1 lieutenant-colonel, 1 captain, 4 horses, wounded; 1 staff, 1 serjeant, 1 horse, missing.

2nd Battalion 1st Royal Regiment—1 subaltern, 9 rank and file, missing.

25th Regiment—14 rank and file missing.

79th Regiment—2 serjeants, 8 rank and file, missing.

92nd Regiment—4 rank and file missing.

Total—15 horses killed; 1 lieutenant-colonel, 1 captain, 4 horses, wounded; 1 subaltern, 1 staff, 3 serjeants, 35 rank and file, 1 horse, missing. N.B.—The wounded men left in Egmont-op-Zee are included under the head of " Missing."

No. 13.

General Order issued by the Duke of York, on the occasion of the Retreat from Alkmaar.

Headquarters, Schagenbrug, Oct. 8th.

Parole—*Portsmouth*; Countersign—*St Peter's.'*

His Royal Highness the Commander-in-Chief desires the troops will accept his best thanks for the persevering bravery and good order which have so eminently distinguished their conduct during the whole period from the 2nd to the 8th past, although suffering from the inclemency of the weather and precarious supplies, necessarily originating out of the situation of the army. From the former of these two causes. His Royal Highness has found it necessary to withdraw the troops from a situation where they must have been continually exposed to insupportable hardships, and which no efforts of an enemy twice beaten could have effected.